A BOOK

OF

MARRIAGE

a

A BOOK
OF
MARRIAGE

SELECTED AND WITH A FOREWORD BY
IVOR BROWN

DECORATED BY
WILLIAM McLAREN

HAMISH HAMILTON
LONDON

First published in Great Britain, 1963
by Hamish Hamilton Ltd.
90 Great Russell Street London WC 1
Copyright © 1963 by Ivor Brown

Printed in Great Britain by
T. & A. Constable Ltd.
Hopetoun Street Edinburgh

TO
MY WIFE

ACKNOWLEDGMENTS

Acknowledgments are due to the following for giving permission to quote: Chatto and Windus Ltd., for the extract from *Do What You Will* by Aldous Huxley;

William Collins, Sons and Co. Ltd., for a poem from *Collected Poems* by Edmund Blunden;

J. M. Dent & Sons Ltd., for extracts from the Everyman Library edition of *The Diary of a Nobody* by George and Weedon Grossmith;

Harvard College Library, Cambridge, Massachusetts, for the letter from Keats to Fanny Brawne;

Jarrolds Publishers (London) Ltd., for the extract from *Sunset Song* by Lewis Grassic Gibbon;

John Murray Ltd., for the extract from *The Sign of Four* by Arthur Conan Doyle, and for the poem "From a Surrey Garden" from John Betjeman's *Collected Poems*;

Penguin Books Ltd., for the extract from Professor Nevile Coghill's translation of *The Canterbury Tales*;

The Public Trustee and The Society of Authors, for extracts from *Getting Married*, *Candida* and *Man and Superman* by George Bernard Shaw;

Major Sir Ralph Verney, Bart., for letters (from the Verney manuscripts at Claydon House) quoted in Sir Arthur Bryant's *Postman's Horn*;

A. P. Watt and Son and the Executors of the late H. G. Wells, for extract from *Love and Mr. Lewisham*.

CONTENTS

PART TWO

THE WEDDING DAY

PART THREE

LATER ON

PART FOUR

OPINION AND ADVICE

In making my choices for this anthology of married life, I have
included the approach to as well as the achievement of such a
partnership. But wooing is only given its place when a wedding
is mentioned or clearly intended. This rules out the vast
quantity of admirable writing, in various forms of our language,
in which the beauties and virtues of the loved one are praised
without declaration of purpose. Much of this may have been
as ethical as it was lyrical and as much a prelude to a sanctified
or secularly recognised union as any clergyman or registrar of
marriages could wish. Who shall say? But a limit had to be set,
not because I have any wish to be censorious but because it was
necessary to keep so large a subject within some bounds of
quantity. Naturally it is not easy to decide the exact target of
many of the most appreciated songs of devotion and most
poignant appeals to 'live with me and be my love'. Those who
have echoed that request may have had the ring and the
prayer-book in mind; or they may have been thinking that
more bliss could be enjoyed with less bondage.

The matter is further complicated by the wide scope given
in our language to the word Mistress. This can be an alter-
native to the Biblical concubine and a tenant of the affections
unlikely to hold a long lease or it may be used by the most
uxorious. Robert Browning, born in a Noncomformist family
and in his later years described by Aldous Huxley as 'that
infinitely respectable rebel and profoundly Anglican worshipper of passion' often appealed to his Mistress, not only when
he was speaking for others as the author of Dramatic Lyrics
but as a man adoring. He is obviously addressing under this
title his Elizabeth, intensely beloved in marriage as in courtship. When she in turn wrote Sonnets of Love it is plain that
she had in mind her rescuer from the invalid's couch in
Wimpole Street, the husband who remained the ruler-partner
of her mind and heart. Mistress was long a usual name for one

honourably wooed and contracted; it was shortened and demeaned as Mrs. or the common Missus. The Scots, to some extent, retain the old and gracious usage. It pleases my wife, when in Scotland, to be addressed as Mistress Brown.

The praise of love down the centuries has been of such boundless volume as well as beauty that it is no handicap but a relief to the anthologist to have his boundaries fixed. My practice has been to be as widely inclusive as possible within the sphere of matrimony, the approach to it, and its aftermath. All moods were to be accepted. Concerning marriage as an institution the comments of the reformer and the cynic have been set beside the happy sentiments of the satisfied and the opinions of the conventional moralist. Of the Wedding Day and its rites and revels I have set the raptures of the Epithalamy beside the sometimes acid humours of the descriptive reporter.

To limit the field further I have chosen, with one exception, poems and passages of prose written in the language of British, Irish, and American writers. If one includes translations the territory becomes an immeasurable continent. The breach of this rule was made in the case of Sir Thomas Urquhart who, as his exponent Mr. D. B. Wyndham Lewis rightly says, did not so much translate Rabelais as transmute him. He added his own plentiful decorations to the descriptions which he most relished and his version of Gargantuan proceedings was as much a new enrichment of our language as a tribute to the fancy and gusto of the French.

Anthologists, whatever the subjects they choose for their gathering of rose-buds or bitter herbs, commonly include the well-known with some unfamiliar selections prized by themselves. Many readers feel deprived if the writing which is popular on its merits is discarded simply because of its popularity. To omit the excellent because it has given general pleasure may be a form of intellectual arrogance. What Disraeli said of politics, that 'a majority is always the best repartee', has some validity in literature and is certainly a consolation to the author who continues to be critically kicked down stairs because he or she once wrote a best-seller. But the service of the compact majority by inclusion of the 'anthology favourite' must be tempered with the provision of excerpts from work which those who are not of the widest reading may find fresh and rewarding. At least—that is one's hope.

It would have been easy to pack this book with extracts from one author alone since wooings and weddings are frequent in the plays of Shakespeare. But in this case the familiarity with certain pieces is so general and their place in the schools' curriculum has been so universal that it seemed better to restrict his share of the whole ('Oh withered is the garland'— of the class-room) and make a few selections which, though familiar since all Shakespeare is familiar, are probably less repeated than most. I therefore decided to take 'Romeo and Juliet' and 'Twelfth Night' as having been read, recited, and seen and heard in the theatre on the widest scale and to give their splendours a rest. As to time of composition I have drawn on the centuries since Chaucer set his Wife of Bath so saltily defending marriage as a good habit and as something worthily earning plentiful repetition with divine sanction if husbands be conveniently short-lived. In so planning my chosen words I have endeavoured to meet the welcome suggestion of my publisher and to do justice to the richness of a theme which has appropriately provided a labour of love for myself.

IVOR BROWN

PART ONE

WOOING

RING TIME

It was a lover and his lass,
  With a hey, and a ho, and a hey nonino,
That o'er the green corn-field did pass
  In spring-time, the only pretty ring-time,
When birds do sing, hey ding a ding, ding;
Sweet lovers love the spring.

Between the acres of the rye,
  With a hey, and a ho, and a hey nonino,
These pretty country-folks would lie
  In spring-time, etc.

This carol they began that hour,
  With a hey, and a ho, and a hey nonino,
How that a life was but a flower
  In spring-time, etc.

And therefore take the present time,
  With a hey, and a ho, and a hey nonino;
For love is crowned with the prime
  In spring-time, the only pretty ring-time,
When birds do sing, hey ding a ding, ding:
Sweet lovers love the spring.

WILLIAM SHAKESPEARE (1564–1616)
As You Like it, Act V, Scene III

THE DAYS BEFORE THE DAY

The uneasy married life of Thomas and Jane Welsh Carlyle was preceded by five years of lengthy and often lively correspondence. The wedding was in October, 1826. Here are their last letters before what he called 'the buckling'.

Miss Welsh to T. Carlyle, Scotsbrig.

Templand, Tuesday, 3 Oct. 1826.

Unkind that you are ever to suffer me to be cast down, when it is so easy a thing for you to lift me to the Seventh Heaven! My soul was darker than midnight, when your pen said 'let there be light', and there *was* light as at the bidding of the Word. And now I am resolved in spirit and even joyful, —joyful even in the face of the dreaded ceremony, of *starvation*,[1] and every possible fate. Oh, my dearest Friend! be always *so* good to me, and I shall make the best and happiest Wife. When I read in your books and words that you love me, I feel it in the deepest part of my soul; then I care not one straw for the whole Universe beside; but when you fly from my caresses to—smoke tobacco, or speak of me as a new *circumstance* of your lot, then indeed my 'heart is troubled about many things'.

My Mother is not come yet, but is expected this week; the week following must be given to her to take a last look at her Child; and then, Dearest, God willing, I am your own for ever and ever.

This day fortnight would suit *me* better than Thursday; for, you know, after the proclaiming one is not fit to be seen, and therefore the sooner we get away the better. But then it would not suit—the Carriers?—unless, perhaps you could send your things the week before, or leave them to follow after you. However, the difference of two days is of no such moment

---

[1] Thomas Carlyle was not earning much at the time.

in my mind that you may not fix whichever *you* find most convenient. So determine and let me know.

With respect to the proclamation, I am grieved to say I can give you no comfort; for not only must you be proclaimed like any common man, in your own Parish, but send a line from the Minister certifying you *unmarried*, before they will proclaim us here. Mr. Anderson, for his own part, would require nothing of the sort; but his Elders, he says, are mighty sticklish about forms. They would not register the marriage unless it were gone about in the regular way.—It is a pity! But, after all, the *crying*[1] is the least of it.

Will you and John come here the night before, or not? Whichever way you like. If you come, I have a notion I will not see you; but I cannot say positively at this distance. Oh mercy! What I would give to be sitting in our doll's-house, married for a week!

Have you spoken to Jane yet about coming to us? and will she trust herself to my sisterly care? I would not have her for a month or two,—till I have got over the first awkwardness of such a change, and my wits are recovered from the bewilderment of the new world about me, sufficiently to look to her welfare. Surely we should feel happier for having the good, little creature with us; and the arrangement, I trust, would not be without benefit to herself. For my own share in it, I engage to be a true kind Sister to her, and an instructor as far as I can. Tell her this, if you see good; and give her a kiss in my name. I may well return *one* out of *twenty*. But indeed, Dear, these kisses on paper are scarce worth keeping. You gave me one on my neck that night you were in such good-humour, and one on my lips on some forgotten occasion, that I would not part with for a hundred thousand paper ones. Perhaps some day or other, I shall get none of either sort: *sic transit gloria mundi.*

There came a Letter from my pretty Cousin, Phoebe Baillie, the other night, almost sentimental, for a wonder. The Girl has taken it into her head, and not without reason

[1] Of the banns.

that my grave Helpmate will hardly be able to endure her; so she conjures us, in all seriousness, not to discard her utterly, and thereby blast her hopes of ever becoming more wise! You will surely let me teach her German, Dear? I promised, and you would not have me break my word. Besides the poor little soul has none to speak one true word to her but only me; and her follies, I would fain persuade myself, are more of education than of nature. But you shall see her in good time, and judge for yourself; and then, not my will be done, but thine. I am going to be really a very meek-tempered Wife. Indeed, I am begun to be meek-tempered already. My Aunt tells me she could live forever with *me* without quarrelling,— I am so reasonable and equal in my humour. There is something to gladden your heart withal! And more than this; my Grandfather observed while I was supping my porridge last night, that 'she was really a douce peaceable body that *Pen*!' So you perceive, my good Sir, the fault will be wholly your own, if we do not get on most harmoniously together.—My Grandfather has been down stairs on Sunday evening, I found him poring over *Wilhelm Meister*! 'A strange choice,' I observed by way of taking the first word with him, 'for Sunday reading.' But he answered me quite sharply, 'Not at all, Miss; the Book is a very *good* Book: it is all about David and Goliath!'—But I must stop. And this is my last Letter! What a thought! How terrible, and yet full of bliss! You will love me forever, will you not, my own Husband? and I will always be your true and affectionate

Jane Welsh

T. Carlyle to Miss Baillie Welsh, Templand.
Scotsbrig, Monday-night, 9 October, 1826.

'The Last Speech and *marrying* words of that unfortunate young woman Jane Baillie *Welsh*,' I received on Friday-morning; and truly a most delightful and swan-like melody was in them; a tenderness and warm devoted trust, worthy of such a maiden bidding farewell to the (unmarried) Earth, of which she was the fairest ornament. Dear little Child! How is it that I have deserved thee; deserved a purer and nobler heart than falls to the lot of millions? I swear I will love thee with *my* whole heart, and think my life well spent if it can make thine happy.

In fine, these preliminaries are in the way towards adjustment. After some vain galloping and consultation, I have at length got that certificate which the Closeburn Session in their sapience deem necessary; I have ordered the Proclaiming of Banns in this Parish of Middlebie, and written out a Note giving order for it in your Parish of Closeburn. Pity, by the way, that there is no man in the Closeburn Church possessed of any little fraction of vulgar earthly logic! It might have saved me a ride to Hoddam Manse this morning (the good Yorstoun my native Parson was away), and a most absurd application to the 'glass Minister' my neighbour. One would think that after fair *crying* three times through the organs of Archibald Blacklock, this certificate of celibacy would be like gilding refined gold, or adding a perfume to the violet: for would not my existing wife, in case I had one, forthwith, at the first hum from Archibald's windpipe, start up in her place, and state aloud that *she* had 'objections'?—But I will not quarrel with these Reverend men; *laissez les faire*, they will buckle us fast enough at length, and for the *How* I care not.

Your own day, Tuesday, as was fitting, I have made mine. Jack and I will surely call on Monday evening at Templand, most likely *after* tea; but I think it will be more commodious for all parties that we sleep at the Inn. You will not see me on Monday-night? I bet two to one you will! At all events I hope you will on Tuesday; so, as Jack says, 'it is much the same'.

All hands are sorting, packing, rummaging and rioting here. To Jane I read her part of your Letter; she will accompany us in our Edinburgh sojourn with all the pleasure in the world. Jack will bring her out, when we want her: she may try the household for awhile; if it suit she will have cause to love her Sister for her life long.

Your Mother will take down this Note to the Minister, and appoint the hour? I think, it should be an early one, for we have far to go. Perhaps also she might do something towards engaging post-horses at the Inn; but I suppose there is little fear of failure in that point.

Do you know aught of wedding-gloves? I must leave all that to you; for except a vague tradition of some such thing I am profoundly ignorant concerning the whole matter. Or will you give *any*? *Ach du guter Gott!* Would we were off and away, three-months before all these observances of the Ceremonial Law!

Yet fear not, Darling; for it must and will be all accomplished, and I admitted to thy bosom and thy heart, and we two made *one life* in the sight of God and man! O my own Jane! I could say much; and what were words to the sea of thoughts that rolls thro' my heart, when I feel that thou art mine, that I am thine, that henceforth we live not for ourselves but for each other! Let us pray to God that our holy purposes be not frustrated; let us trust in Him and in each other, and fear no evil that can befall us. My last blessing as a Lover is with you; this is my last Letter to Jane Welsh: my first blessing as a Husband, my first kiss to Jane Carlyle is at hand! O my Darling! I will always love thee.

Good night, then, for the last time we have to part! In a week I see you, in a week you are my own! *Adieu Meine Eigene!*

In haste, I am forever yours,

T. Carlyle

JANE WELSH CARLYLE (1801–1866)
THOMAS CARLYLE (1795–1881)
Letters

A WORD FOR THE WIDOW

The Widow can bake, and the Widow can brew,
The Widow can shape, and the Widow can shew,
And mony braw Things the Widow can do;
    Then have at the Widow, my Laddie.
With Courage attack her baith early and late,
To kiss her and clap her ye mauna be blate:[1]
Speak well, and do better; for that's the best Gate[2]
    To win a young Widow, my Laddie.

The Widow she's youthfu', and never ae Hair
The war[3] of the wearing, and has a good Skair[4]
Of everything lovely; she's witty and fair,
    And has a rich Jointure, my Laddie.
What cou'd ye wish better your Pleasure to crown,
Than a Widow, the bonniest Toast in the Town,
With nathing, but draw in your Stool, and sit down,
    And sport with the Widow, my Laddie!

Then till her, and kill her with Courtesy dead,
Tho' stark Love and Kindness be all ye can plead;
Be heartsome and airy, and hope to succeed
    With a bonny gay Widow, my Laddie.
Strike Iron while 'tis het, if ye'd have it to wald,[5]
For Fortune ay favours the Active and Bauld,
But ruines the Woer that's thowless[6] and cauld,
    Unfit for the Widow, my Laddie.

ALLAN RAMSAY (1686–1758)
Poems

---

[1] Bashful.   [2] Way.   [3] Worse.
[4] Share.   [5] Wield.   [6] Inert.

DEVOTION, BUT IN VAIN

To Mistress Mary Eure from Edmund Verney.

12 April, 1658.

Madam,

You are so perfect empress of my heart that in obedience to yours by Mr. Butterfield, I have used more violence upon myself these three weeks than a Russe who takes it for an honour to destroy himself at his Prince's command. For my affection is so pure that it carries with it an absolute resignation of myself to you though with my own destruction, and in conformity to your order, I believed that you were then best enjoyed by me when I wrought your greatest content. Believe me (Madam) this zeal hath forced me out of myself, as far as any saint ever was, in a rapture; yet after all my art and diligence to put this candle under a bushel, it burnt the more furiously, because I tried so much to extinguish it. For I protest before the majesty of God, I find by strong experience that I can no more obtain of my will to abate of your love than I can of my memory that there is no such person as you are, or my understanding that you are not adorned with all those perfections, the idea whereof doth so possess and ravish my soul.

I vow by your supremacy and my allegiance that I can ascribe the growth of my love to this vast height to no other cause but your huge merit, and my great care not to sin against it through unadvisedness or indiscretion. This made me study how to compose my father's displeasure, and answer your lady mother's scruples and your desire of single life, before I totally submitted to the sweet conquest your goodness hath over me. To which I am now so complete a captive that all the neglect you can fasten on your slave, or the diversion friends can prompt me to, are able to beget no other thought in me than of living and dying your devotee. Wherefore I beseech you to consider how it can become your nature, so full of grace and goodness, to call me not Naomi but Marah, for the Lord hath dealt bitterly with me and the waters of Marah are bitter to your supplicant by giving bitterness of spirit to that heart which begs your compassion and comfort. Your own knowledge of the integrity thereof cannot but tell you this deserves not the corrosive of a denial, and my faith and knowledge of your candour and sweetness assure me that no words so harsh can fall from your tongue or pen.

I beseech you to give me leave to add one grain of reason to all this weight of affection, which is that your resolution is contrary to that end whereto God and nature ordained you: not regardful to your dearest relations dead and living, but above all injurious to yourself. . . . If you put my affection in one scale and your resolution in the other, and if only judgment held the balance (which I reasonably hope kindness may somewhat bias) I shall not be condemned for prizing this so great and well-grounded truth that it is impossible for me to live or die other than, Madam, sweetest lady,

Your most passionately devoted vassal,

EDMUND VERNEY

To the Hon. Mrs. Sherard from her daughter, Mary Eure.
8 May, 1658.

Madam,

Be pleased to accept my humblest duty and to know that since you left Whitsuntide I have received a wandering letter from my cousin Edmund Verney. How it came to Melton I know not, but there Joseph found it. Really I was never more surprised in my life, for I thought my last to his might have prevented his farther troubling himself. For since you have always been pleased to leave me to myself I could wish he knew that if he write or speak a thousand times it will not prevail with me at all. I am sorry he forceth me to say, if I would marry it should not be him. Not that I have anything against my cousin, but esteem him as he is my near relation. But never whilst I breathe will I be wrought to have the least thought of giving him any encouragement in his pretensions. He would much oblige me to leave persisting in it.

Madam, I shall not answer his letter without your command, which I hope I shall not receive because I should unwillingly obey it. All the acknowledgement in the world I render you for your long past promise of never persuading me to marry. Sweet Madam, that is my resolution; when I change it, your Ladyship shall know, but I believe I shall never trouble you with that message. Be pleased to pardon this long impertinency and grant me your blessing. Thus I remain, Dear Madam,

your obedient daughter,

MARY EURE

Quoted from Sir Arthur Bryant's anthology of seventeenth-century letters called *Postman's Horn*, with kind permission of Sir Ralph Verney, Bart. The unhappy Edmund Verney did find a wife and let us hope happiness four years later.

LOVE IN THE VALLEY

Under yonder beech-tree standing on the green-sward,
Crouch'd with her arms behind her little head,
Her knees folded up, and her tresses on her bosom,
  Lies my young love sleeping in the shade.
Had I the heart to slide an arm beneath her,
  Press her dreaming lips as her waist I folded slow,
Waking on the instant she could not but embrace me—
  Ah! would she hold me, and never let me go?

Shy as the squirrel, and wayward as the swallow;
  Swift as the swallow when athwart the western flood
Circleting the surface he meets his mirrored winglets,—
  Is that dear one in her maiden bud.
Shy as the squirrel whose nest is the pine-tops;
  Gentle—ah! that she were jealous as the dove!
Full of all the wildness of the woodland creatures,
  Happy in herself is the maiden that I love!

What can have taught her distrust of all I tell her?
  Can she truly doubt me when looking on my brows?
Nature never teaches distrust of tender love-tales,
  What can have taught her distrust of all my vows?
No, she does not doubt me! on a dewy eve-tide
  Whispering together beneath the listening moon,
I pray'd till her cheek flush'd, implored till she faltered—
  Fluttered to my bosom—ah! to fly away so soon!

When her mother tends her before the laughing mirror,
  Tying up her laces, looping up her hair,
Often she thinks—were this wild thing wedded,
  I should have more love, and much less care.

When her mother tends her before the bashful mirror,
  Loosening her laces, combing down her curls,
Often she thinks—were this wild thing wedded,
  I should lose but one for so many boys and girls.

Clambering roses peep into her chamber,
  Jasmine and woodbine breathe, sweet, sweet,
White-necked swallows twittering of summer,
  Fill her with balm and nested peace from head to feet.
Ah! will the rose-bough see her lying lonely,
  When the petals fall and fierce bloom is on the leaves?
Will the Autumn garners see her still ungathered,
  When the fickle swallows forsake the weeping eaves?

Comes a sudden question—should a strange hand pluck her?
  Oh! what an anguish smites me at the thought.
Should some idle lordling bribe her mind with jewels!—
  Can such beauty ever thus be bought?
Sometimes the huntsmen prancing down the valley
  Eye the village lasses, full of sprightly mirth;
They see as I see, mine is the fairest!
  Would she were older and could read my worth!

Are there not sweet maidens if she still deny me?
  Show the bridal heavens but one bright star?
Wherefore thus then do I chase a shadow,
  Clattering one note like a brown eve-jar?
So I rhyme and reason till she darts before me—
  Thro' the milky meadows from flower to flower she flies,
Sunning her sweet palms to shade her dazzled eye-lids
  From the golden love that looks too eager in her eyes.

When at dawn she wakens, and her fair face gazes
  Out on the weather thro' the window-panes,
Beauteous she looks! like a white water-lily
  Bursting out of bud on the rippled river plains.

When from bed she rises clothed from neck to ankle
  In her long nightgown, sweet as boughs of May,
Beauteous she looks! like a tall garden lily
  Pure from the night and perfect for the day!

Happy, happy time, when the grey star twinkles
  Over the fields all fresh with bloomy dew;
When the cold-cheeked dawn grows ruddy up the twilight,
  And the gold sun wakes, and weds her in the blue.
Then when my darling tempts the early breezes,
  She the only star that dies not with the dark!
Powerless to speak all the ardour of my passion
  I catch her little hand as we listen to the lark.

Shall the birds in vain then valentine their sweet-hearts?
  Season after season tell a fruitless tale;
Will not the virgin listen to their voices?
  Take the honeyed meaning, wear the bridal veil?
Fears she frosts of winter, fears she the bare branches?
  Waits she the garlands of spring for her dower?
Is she a nightingale that will not be nested
  Till the April woodland has built her bridal bower?

Then come merry April with all thy birds and beauties!
  With thy crescent brows and thy flowery, showery glee;
With thy budding leafage and fresh green pastures;
  And may thy lustrous crescent grow a honeymoon for me!
Come merry month of the cuckoo and the violet!
  Come sweeping Loveliness in all thy blue delight!
Lo! the nest is ready, let me not languish longer!
  Bring her to my arms on the first May night.

GEORGE MEREDITH (1828–1909)
Poems Written in Early Youth

This is the earlier and shorter version of the poem which Meredith later
amplified and perhaps improved. It has been chosen for this anthology because
the revision laid far less stress on the matrimonial side of the lover's adoration.

GOOD SENSE BEFORE GOOD LOOKS

Dr. Johnson married in 1735 the widow of Henry Porter, a Birmingham merchant.

Miss Porter told me, that when he was first introduced to her mother, his appearance was very forbidding: he was then lean and lank, so that his immense structure of bones was hideously striking to the eye, and the scars of the scrophula were deeply visible. He also wore his hair, which was straight and stiff, and separated behind; and he often had, seemingly, convulsive starts and odd gesticulations, which tended to excite at once surprize and ridicule. Mrs. Porter was so much engaged by his conversation that she overlooked all these external disadvantages, and said to her daughter, 'this is the most sensible man that I ever saw in my life'.

JAMES BOSWELL (1740–1795)
The Life of Samuel Johnson

ENGAGED!—CRANFORD'S LADIES AGHAST

———◦〰◦———

We were sitting—Miss Matty and I—much as usual, she in the blue chintz easy-chair, with her back to the light, and her knitting in her hand, I reading aloud the St. James's Chronicle. A few minutes more, and we should have gone to make the little alterations in dress usual before calling-time (twelve o'clock) in Cranford. I remember the scene and the date well. We had been talking of the signor's rapid recovery since the warmer weather had set in, and praising Mr. Hoggins's skill, and lamenting his want of refinement and manner (it seems a curious coincidence that this should have been our subject, but so it was), when a knock was heard—a caller's knock—three distinct taps—and we were flying (that is to say, Miss Matty could not walk very fast, having had a touch of rheumatism) to our rooms, to change cap and collars, when Miss Pole arrested us by calling out, as she came up the stairs, 'Don't go—I can't wait—it is not twelve, I know—but never mind your dress—I must speak to you.'

We did our best to look as if it was not we who had made the hurried movement, the sound of which she had heard; for, of course, we did not like to have it supposed that we had any old clothes that it was convenient to wear out in the 'sanctuary of home', as Miss Jenkyns once prettily called the back parlour, where she was tying up preserves. So we threw our gentility with double force into our manners, and very genteel we were for two minutes while Miss Pole recovered breath, and excited our curiosity strongly by lifting up her hands in amazement, and bringing them down in silence, as if what she had to say was too big for words, and could only be expressed by pantomime.

'What do you think, Miss Matty? What *do* you think?

B

Lady Glenmire is to marry—is to be married, I mean—Lady Glenmire—Mr. Hoggins—Mr. Hoggins is going to marry Lady Glenmire!'

'Marry!' said we. 'Marry! Madness!'

'Marry!' said Miss Pole, with the decision that belonged to her character. '*I* said marry! as you do; and I also said, "What a fool my lady is going to make of herself!" I could have said "Madness!" but I controlled myself, for it was in a public shop that I heard of it. Where feminine delicacy is gone to, I don't know! You and I, Miss Matty, would have been ashamed to have known that our marriage was spoken of in a grocer's shop, in the hearing of shopmen!'

'But,' said Miss Matty, sighing as one recovering from a blow, 'perhaps it is not true. Perhaps we are doing her injustice.'

'No,' said Miss Pole. 'I have taken care to ascertain that. I went straight to Mrs. Fitz-Adam, to borrow a cookery book which I knew she had; and I introduced my congratulations *à propos* of the difficulty gentlemen must have in housekeeping; and Mrs. Fitz-Adam bridled up, and said that she believed it was true, though how and where I could have heard it she did not know. She said her brother and Lady Glenmire had come to an understanding at last. "Understanding!" such a coarse word! But my lady will have to come down to many a want of refinement. I have reason to believe Mr. Hoggins sups on bread-and-cheese and beer every night.'

'Marry!' said Miss Matty once again. 'Well! I never thought of it. Two people that we know going to be married. It's coming very near!'

'So near that my heart stopped beating, when I heard of it, while you might have counted twelve,' said Miss Pole.

'One does not know whose turn may come next. Here, in Cranford, poor Lady Glenmire might have thought herself safe,' said Miss Matty, with a gentle pity in her tones.

'Bah!' said Miss Pole, with a toss of her head. 'Don't you remember poor dear Captain Brown's song "Tibbie Fowler," and the line—

"Set her on the Tintock Tap,
    The wind will blaw a man till her." '

'That was because "Tibbie Fowler" was rich, I think.'

'Well! there is a kind of attraction about Lady Glenmire that I, for one, should be ashamed to have.'

I put in my wonder. 'But how can she have fancied Mr. Hoggins? I am not surprised that Mr. Hoggins has liked her.'

'Oh! I don't know. Mr. Hoggins is rich, and very pleasant-looking,' said Miss Matty, 'and very good-tempered and kind-hearted.'

'She has married for an establishment, that's it. I suppose she takes the surgery with it,' said Miss Pole, with a little dry laugh at her own joke. But, like many people who think they have made a severe and sarcastic speech, which yet is clever of its kind, she began to relax in her grimness from the moment when she made this allusion to the surgery; and we turned to speculate on the way in which Mrs. Jamieson would receive the news. The person whom she had left in charge of her house to keep off followers from her maids to set up a follower of her own! And that follower a man whom Mrs. Jamieson had tabooed as vulgar, and inadmissible to Cranford society, not merely account of his name, but because of his voice, his complexion, his boots, smelling of the stable, and himself, smelling of drugs. Had he ever been to see Lady Glenmire at Mrs. Jamieson's? Chloride of lime would not purify the house in its owner's estimation if he had. Or had their interviews been confined to the occasional meeting in the chamber of the poor sick conjuror, to whom, with all our sense of the *mésalliance*, we could not help allowing that they had both been exceedingly kind? And now it turned out that a servant of Mrs. Jamieson's had been ill, and Mr. Hoggins had been attending her for some weeks. So the wolf had got into the fold, and now he was carrying off the shepherdess. What would Mrs. Jamieson say?

*

I don't know whether it is a fancy of mine, or a real fact, but I have noticed that, just after the announcement of an engagement in any set, the unmarried ladies in that set flutter out in an unusual gaiety and newness of dress, as much as to say, in a tacit and unconscious manner, 'We also are spinsters'. Miss Matty and Miss Pole talked and thought more about bonnets, gowns, caps, and shawls, during the fortnight that succeeded this call, than I had known them do for years before. But it might be the spring weather, for it was a warm and pleasant March; and merinoes and beavers, and woollen materials of all sorts were but ungracious receptacles of the bright sun's glancing rays.

It had not been Lady Glenmire's dress that had won Mr. Hoggins's heart, for she went about on her errands of kindness more shabby than ever. Although in the hurried glimpses I caught of her at church or elsewhere she appeared rather to shun meeting any of her friends, her face seemed to have almost something of the flush of youth in it; her lips looked redder and more trembling full than in their old compressed state, and her eyes dwelt on all things with a lingering light, as if she was learning to love Cranford and its belongings. Mr. Hoggins looked broad and radiant, and creaked up the middle aisle at church in a brand-new pair of top-boots—an audible, as well as visible, sign of his purposed change of state; for the tradition went, that the boots he had worn till now were the identical pair in which he first set out on his rounds in Cranford twenty-five years ago; only they had been new-pieced, high and low, top and bottom, heel and sole, black leather and brown leather, more times than any one could tell.

None of the ladies in Cranford chose to sanction the marriage by congratulating either of the parties. We wished to ignore the whole affair until our liege lady, Mrs. Jamieson, returned. Till she came back to give us our cue, we felt that it would be better to consider the engagement in the same light as the Queen of Spain's legs—facts which certainly existed, but the less said about the better.

MRS. GASKELL (1810–1865)
Cranford, Chapter XII

DEMURRERS IN LOVE

As my correspondents upon the subjects of love are very numerous, it is my design, if possible, to range them under several heads, and address myself to them at different times. The first branch of them, to whose service I shall dedicate this paper, are those that have to do with women of dilatory tempers, who are for spinning out the time of courtship to an immoderate length, without being able either to close with their lovers or to dismiss them.

Among all my plaintiffs of this nature, I most pity the unfortunate Philander, a man of a constant passion and plentiful fortune, who sets forth, that the timorous and irresolute Sylvia has demurred till she is past child-bearing. Strephon appears by his letter to be a very choleric lover, and irrevocably smitten with one that demurs out of self-interest. He tells me with great passion, that she has bubbled him out of his youth; that she drilled him on to five-and-fifty; and that he verily believes she will drop him in his old age if she can find her account in another. I shall conclude this narrative with a letter from honest Sam. Hopewell, a very pleasant fellow, who it seems has at last married a demurrer: I must only premise, that Sam, who is a very good bottle companion, has been the diversion of his friends, upon account of his passion, ever since the year one thousand six hundred and eighty-one.

Dear Sir,

You know very well my passion for Mrs. Martha, and what a dance she has led me: she took me out at the age of two-and-twenty, and dodged with me above thirty years. I have loved her till she is grown as grey as a cat, and am with much ado become the master of her person, such as it is at present. She is, however, in my eye, a very charming old woman. We often lament that we did not marry sooner, but she has nobody to blame for it but herself. You know very well that she would never think of me whilst she had a tooth in her head. I have put the date of my passion, (*Anno Amoris trigesimo primo,*) instead of a posie, on my wedding-ring. I expect you should send me a congratulatory letter; or, if you please, an epithalamium, upon this occasion.

Mrs. Martha's and your eternally,

Sam. Hopewell

In order to banish an evil out of the world, that does not only produce great uneasiness to private persons, but has also a very bad influence on the public, I shall endeavour to show the folly of demurring, from two or three reflections, which I earnestly recommend to the thoughts of my fair readers.

First of all, I would have them seriously think on the shortness of their time. Life is not long enough for a coquette to play all her tricks in. A timorous woman drops into her grave before she has done deliberating. Were the age of man the same that it was before the flood, a lady might sacrifice half a century to a scruple, and be two or three ages in demurring. Had she nine hundred years good, she might hold out to the conversion of the Jews before she thought fit to be prevailed upon. But, alas! she ought to play her part in haste, when she considers that she is suddenly to quit the stage, and make room for others.

In the second place, I would desire my female readers to consider, that as the term of life is short, that of beauty is much shorter. The finest skin wrinkles in a few years, and loses the strength of its colouring so soon, that we have scarce time to admire it. I might embellish this subject with roses and rainbows, and several other ingenious conceits, which I may possibly reserve for another opportunity.

There is a third consideration, which I would likewise recommend to a demurrer, and that is, the great danger of her falling in love when she is about three-score, if she cannot satisfy her doubts and scruples before that time. There is a kind of latter spring, that sometimes gets into the blood of an old woman, and turns her into a very odd sort of an animal. I would therefore have the demurrer consider what a strange figure she will make, if she chances to get over all difficulties, and comes to a final resolution, in that unseasonable part of her life.

I would not, however, be understood by anything I have here said, to discourage that natural modesty in the sex, which renders a retreat from the first approaches of a lover both fashionable and graceful; all that I intend is, to advise them, when they are prompted by reason and inclination, to demur only out of form, and so far as decency requires. A virtuous woman should reject the first offer of marriage, as a good man does that of a bishopric; but I would advise neither the one nor the other to persist in refusing what they secretly approve.

JOSEPH ADDISON (1672–1719)
Essays

FROM A SURREY GARDEN

Miles of pram in the wind and Pam in the gorse track,
  Coco-nut smell of the broom, and a packet of Weights
Press'd in the sand. The thud of a hoof on a horse-track—
    A horse-riding horse for a horse-track—
    Conifer county of Surrey approached
  Through remarkable wrought-iron gates.

Over your boundary now, I wash my face in a bird-bath,
  Then which path shall I take? that over there by the pram?
Down by the pond! or—yes, I will take the slippery third path,
    Trodden away with gym shoes,
    Beautiful fir-dry alley that leads
To the bountiful body of Pam.

Pam, I adore you, Pam, you great big mountainous sports girl,
  Whizzing them over the net, full of the strength of five:
That old Malvernian brother, you zephyr and khaki shorts girl,
    Although he's playing for Woking,
    Can't stand up
To your wonderful backhand drive.

See the strength of her arm, as firm and hairy as Hendren's;
  See the size of her thighs, the pout of her lips as, cross,
And full of a pent-up strength, she swipes at the rhododen-
                                                drons,
    Lucky the rhododendrons,
    And flings her arrogant love-lock
Back with a petulant toss.

Over the redolent pinewoods, in at the bathroom casement,
  One fine Saturday, Windlesham bells shall call:
Up the Butterfield aisle rich with Gothic enlacement,
    Licensed now for embracement,
    Pam and I, as the organ
Thunders over you all.

JOHN BETJEMAN (1906–   )
Collected Poems

PROPOSALS AND PROVISOS

Enter Mirabell to Mrs. Millamant.

Mirabell. 'Like Daphne she, as lovely and as coy.' Do you lock yourself up from me, to make my search more curious? or is this pretty artifice contrived to signify that here the chase must end, and my pursuits be crowned? For you can fly no further.

Mrs. Millamant. Vanity! no—I'll fly, and be followed to the last moment. Though I am upon the very verge of matrimony, I expect you should solicit me as much as if I were wavering at the gate of a monastery, with one foot over the threshold. I'll be solicited to the very last, nay, and afterwards.

Mirabell. What, after the last?

Mrs. Millamant. Oh, I should think I was poor and had nothing to bestow, if I were reduced to an inglorious ease, and freed from the agreeable fatigues of solicitation.

Mirabell. But do not you know, that when favours are conferred upon instant and tedious solicitation, that they diminish in their value, and that both the giver loses the grace, and the receiver lessens his pleasure?

Mrs. Millamant. It may be in things of common application; but never sure in love. Oh, I hate a lover that can dare to think he draws a moment's air, independent of the bounty of his mistress. There is not so impudent a thing in nature, as the saucy look of an assured man, confident of success. The pedantic arrogance of a very husband has not so pragmatical an air. Ah! I'll never marry, unless I am first made sure of my will and pleasure.

Mirabell. Would you have 'em both before marriage? or will you be contented with the first now, and stay for the other till after grace?

Mrs. Millamant. Ah! don't be impertinent.—My dear liberty, shall I leave thee? my faithful solitude, my darling contemplation, must I bid you then adieu? Ay-h adieu—my morning thoughts, agreeable wakings, indolent slumbers, all ye douceurs, ye sommeils du matin, adieu?—I can't do't, 'tis more than impossible—positively, Mirabell, I'll lie abed in a morning as long as I please.

Mirabell. Then I'll get up in a morning as early as I please.

Mrs. Millamant. Ah! idle creature, get up when you will—and d'ye hear, I won't be called names after I'm married; positively I won't be called names.

Mirabell. Names!

Mrs. Millamant. Ay, as wife, spouse, my dear, joy, jewel, love, sweetheart, and the rest of that nauseous cant, in which men and their wives are so fulsomely familiar—I shall never bear that—good Mirabell, don't let us be familiar or fond, nor kiss before folks, like my Lady Fadler and Sir Francis: nor go to Hyde-park together the first Sunday in a new chariot, to provoke eyes and whispers, and then never to be seen there together again; as if we were proud of one another the first week, and ashamed of one another ever after. Let us never visit together, nor go to a play together; but let us be very strange and well-bred: let us be as strange as if we had been married a great while; and as well bred as if we were not married at all.

Mirabell. Have you any more conditions to offer? Hitherto your demands are pretty reasonable.

Mrs. Millamant. Trifles!—As liberty to pay and receive visits to and from whom I please; to write and receive letters, without interrogatories or wry faces on your part; to wear what I please; and choose conversation with regard only to my own taste; to have no obligation upon me to converse with wits that I don't like, because they are your acquaintance: or to be intimate with fools, because they may be your relations. Come to dinner when I please; dine in my dressing-room when I'm out of humour, without giving a reason. To have my closet inviolate; to be sole empress of my tea-table, which you must never presume to approach without first asking leave. And lastly, wherever I am, you shall always knock at the door before you come in. These articles subscribed, if I continue to endure you a little longer, I may by degrees dwindle into a wife.

Mirabell. Your bill of fare is something advanced in this latter account.—Well, have I liberty to offer conditions—that when you are dwindled into a wife, I may not be beyond measure enlarged into a husband?

Mrs. Millamant. You have free leave; propose your utmost, speak and spare not.

Mirabell. I thank you—Imprimis then, I covenant, that your acquaintance be general; that you admit no sworn confidant, or intimate of your own sex; no she friend to screen her affairs under your countenance, and tempt you to make trial of a mutual secrecy. No decoy duck to wheedle you a fop-scrambling to the play in a mask—then bring you home in a pretended fright, when you think you shall be found out—and rail at me for missing the play, and disappointing the frolic which you had to pick me up, and prove my constancy.

Mrs. Millamant. Detestable imprimis! I go to the play in a mask!

Mirabell. Item, I article, that you continue to like your own face, as long as I shall: and while it passes current with me, that you endeavour not to new-coin it. To which end, together with all vizards for the day, I prohibit all masks for the night, made of oiled-skins, and I know not what—hogs' bones, hares' gall, pig-water, and the marrow of a roasted cat. In short, I forbid all commerce with the gentlewoman in what d'ye call it court. Item, I shut my doors against all bawds with baskets, and penny-worths of muslin, china, fans, atlasses, etc. —Item, when you shall be breeding——

*

Mrs. Millamant. Ah! name it not.

Mirabell. Which may be presumed with a blessing on our endeavours.

Mrs. Millamant. Odious endeavours!

Mirabell. I denounce against all strait lacing, squeezing for a shape, till you mould my boy's head like a sugar-loaf, and instead of a man child, make me father to a crooked billet. Lastly, to the dominion of the tea-table I submit—but with proviso, that you exceed not in your province; but restrain yourself to native and simple tea-table drinks, as tea, chocolate, and coffee: as likewise to genuine and authorised tea-table talk—such as mending of fashions, spoiling reputations, railing at absent friends, and so forth—but that on no account you encroach upon the men's prerogative, and presume to drink healths, or toast fellows; for prevention of which I banish all foreign forces, all auxiliaries to the tea-table, as orange-brandy, all aniseed, cinnamon, citron, and Barbadoes waters, together with ratafia, and the most noble spirit of clary—but for cowslip wine, poppy water, and all dormitives, those I allow.— These provisos admitted, in other things I may prove a tractable and complying husband.

Mrs. Millamant. O horrid provisos! filthy strong-waters! I toast fellows! odious men! I hate your odious provisos.

Mirabell. Then we are agreed! shall I kiss your hand upon the contract? And here comes one to be a witness to the sealing of the deed.

WILLIAM CONGREVE (1670–1729)
The Way of the World, Act IV, Scene I

A SOLDIER'S PLEA

(King Henry the Fifth and Princess Katharine of France)

If I could win a lady at leap-frog, or by vaulting into my
saddle with my armour on my back, under the correction of
bragging be it spoken, I should quickly leap into a wife. Or if
I might buffet for my love, or bound my horse for her favours,
I could lay on like a butcher, and sit like a jack-an-apes, never
off. But, before God, Kate, I cannot look greenly, nor gasp
out my eloquence, nor I have no cunning in protestation;
only downright oaths, which I never use till urged, nor never
break for urging. If thou canst love a fellow of this temper,
Kate, whose face is not worth sun-burning, that never looks
in his glass for love of any thing he sees there,—let thine eye
be thy cook. I speak to thee plain soldier: if thou canst love
me for this, take me; if not, to say to thee that I shall die, is
true,—but for thy love, by the Lord, no; yet I love thee too.
And while thou livest, dear Kate, take a fellow of plain and
uncoin'd constancy; for he perforce do thee right, because he
hath not the gift to woo in other places: for these fellows of
infinite tongue, that can rime themselves into ladies' favours,
they do always reason themselves out again. What! a speaker
is but a prater; a rime is but a ballad, A good leg will fall; a
straight back will stoop; a black beard will turn white; a
curl'd pate will grow bald; a fair face will wither; a full eye
will wax hollow: but a good heart, Kate, is the sun and the
moon; or, rather, the sun, and not the moon,—for it shines
bright, and never changes, but keeps his course truly. If thou
would have such a one, take me: and take me, take a soldier;
take a soldier, take a king: and what say'st thou, then, to my
love? speak, my fair, and fairly, I pray thee.

WILLIAM SHAKESPEARE (1564–1616)
King Henry V, Act V, Scene 2

ON THE BRINK

I watch'd her as she stoop'd to pluck
   A wildflower in her hair to twine;
And wish'd that it had been my luck
   To call her mine.

Anon I heard her rate with mad
   Mad words her babe within its cot;
And felt particularly glad
   That it had not.

I knew (such subtle brains have men)
   That she was uttering what she shouldn't;
And thought that I would chide, and then
   I thought I wouldn't:

Who could have gazed upon that face,
   Those pouting coral lips, and chided?
A Rhadamanthus, in my place,
   Had done as I did:

For ire wherewith our bosoms glow
   Is chain'd there oft by Beauty's spell;
And, more than that, I did not know
   The widow well.

So the harsh phrase pass'd unreproved,
   Still mute—(O brothers, was it sin?)—
I drank, unutterably moved,
   Her beauty in:

And to myself I murmur'd low,
   As on her upturn'd face and dress
The moonlight fell, 'Would she say No,
   By chance, or Yes?'

She stood so calm, so like a ghost
   Betwixt me and that magic moon,
That I already was almost
   A finish'd coon.

But when she caught adroitly up
   And soothed with smiles her little daughter;
And gave it, if I'm right, a sup
   Of barley-water;

And, crooning still the strange sweet lore
   Which only mothers' tongues can utter,
Snow'd with deft hand the sugar o'er
   It's bread-and-butter;

And kiss'd it clingingly—(Ah, why
   Don't women do these things in private?)—
I felt that if I lost her, I
   Should not survive it:

And from my mouth the words nigh flew—
   The past, the future, I forgat 'em:
'Oh, if you'd kiss me as you do
   That thankless atom!'

But this thought came ere yet I spake,
   And froze the sentence on my lips:
'They err, who marry wives that make
   Those little slips.'

It came like some familiar rhyme,
   Some copy to my boyhood set;
And that's perhaps the reason I'm
   Unmarried yet.

Would she have own'd how pleased she was,
  And told her love with widow's pride?
I never found out that, because
  I never tried.

Be kind to babes and beasts and birds:
  Hearts may be hard, though lips are coral;
And angry words are angry words:
  And that's the moral.

C. S. CALVERLEY (1831–1884)
Fly Leaves

UNCLE TOBY AND THE WIDOW
——— ᵉᶜᶜ✲ᵔᵔ ———

Tristram Shandy's Uncle Toby courted, with apprehension, the Widow Wadman who, with less reserve courted him. Tristram's father gave this advice to wooers. 'Never go forth upon the enterprise, whether it be in the morning or the afternoon, without first recommending thyself to the protection of Almighty God.' The counsel was not out of place.

Which shows, let your reverences and worships say what you will of it (for as for *thinking*—all who do think—think pretty much alike both upon it and other matters)—Love is certainly, at least alphabetically speaking, one of the most

A gitating
B ewitching
C onfounded
D evilish affairs of life—the most
E xtravagant
F utilitous
G alligaskinish
H andy-dandyish
I racundulous (there is no K to it) and
L yrical of all human passions: at the same time, the most
M isgiving
N innyhammering
O bstipating
P ragmatical
S tridulous
R idiculous—though by the bye the R should have gone first—But in short 'tis such a nature, as my father once told my Uncle *Toby* upon the close of a long dissertation upon the subject—'You can scarce,' said he, 'combine two ideas together upon it, brother *Toby*, without an hypallage'—What's that? cried my uncle *Toby*—

Nothing, quoth my father, but to get in—or let it alone.

Now widow *Wadman*, as I told you before, would do neither the one or the other.

She stood however ready harnessed and caparisoned at all points, to watch accidents.

The Fates, who certainly all foreknew of these amours of widow *Wadman* and my uncle *Toby*, had, from the first creation of matter and motion (and with more courtesy than they usually do things of this kind), established such a chain of causes and effects hanging so fast to one another, that it was scarce possible for my uncle *Toby* to have dwelt in any other house in the world, or to have occupied any other garden in *Christendom*, but the very house and garden which join'd and laid parallel to Mrs. *Wadman's*; this, with the advantage of a thickset arbour in Mrs. *Wadman's* garden, but planted in the hedge-row of my uncle *Toby's*, put all the occasions into her hands which Love-militancy wanted; she could observe my uncle *Toby's* motions, and was mistress likewise of his councils of war; and as his unsuspecting heart had given leave to the corporal, through the mediation of *Bridget*, to make her a wicker-gate of communication to enlarge her walks, it enabled her to carry on her approaches to the very door of the sentry-box; and sometimes out of gratitude, to make an attack, and endeavour to blow up my uncle *Toby* in the very sentry-box itself.

*

—I am half distracted, captain *Shandy*, said Mrs. *Wadman*, holding up her cambrick handkerchief to her left eye, as she approach'd the door of my uncle *Toby's* sentry-box—a mote—or sand—or something—I know not what, has got into this eye of mine—do look into it—it is not in the white—

In saying which, Mrs. *Wadman* edged herself close in beside my uncle *Toby*, and squeezing herself down upon the corner of his bench, she gave him an opportunity of doing it without rising up—Do look into it—said she.

Honest soul! thou didst look into it with as much innocency

of heart, as ever child look'd into a raree-shew-box; and 'twere as much a sin to have hurt thee.

—If a man will be peeping of his own accord into things of that nature—I've nothing to say to it—

My uncle *Toby* never did: and I will answer for him, that he would have sat quietly upon a sofa from *June* to *January* (which, you know, takes in both the hot and cold months), with an eye as fine as the Thracian Rodope's beside him, without being able to tell, whether it was a black or blue one.

The difficulty was to get my uncle *Toby* to look at one at all. 'Tis surmounted. And

I see him yonder with his pipe pendulous in his hand, and the ashes falling out of it—looking—and looking—then rubbing his eyes—and looking again, with twice the good-nature that ever Gallileo look'd for a spot in the sun.

—In vain! for by all the powers which animate the organ —Widow *Wadman's* left eye shines this moment as lucid as her right—there is neither mote, or sand, or dust, or chaff, or speck, or particle of opake matter floating in it—There is nothing, my dear paternal uncle! but one lambent delicious fire, furtively shooting out from every part of it, in all directions into thine—

—If thou lookest, uncle *Toby*, in search of this mote one moment longer—thou art undone.

An eye is for all the world exactly like a cannon, in this respect; That it is not so much the eye or the cannon, in themselves, as it is the carriage of the eye—and the carriage of the cannon, by which both the one and the other are enabled to do so much execution. I don't think the comparison a bad one; However, as 'tis made and placed at the head of the chapter, as much for use as ornament, all I desire in return is, that whenever I speak of Mrs. *Wadman's* eyes (except once in the next period), that you keep it in your fancy.

I protest, Madam, said my uncle *Toby*, I can see nothing whatever in your eye.

It is not in the white; said Mrs. *Wadman*: my uncle *Toby* look'd with might and main into the pupil—

Now of all the eyes which ever were created—from your own, Madam, up to those of *Venus* herself, which certainly were as venereal a pair of eyes as ever stood in a head—there never was an eye of them all, so fitted to rob my uncle *Toby* of his repose, as the very eye, at which he was looking—it was not, Madam, a rolling eye—a romping or a wanton one—nor was it an eye sparkling—petulant or imperious—of high claims and terrifying exactions, which would have curdled at once that milk of human nature, of which my uncle *Toby* was made up—but 'twas an eye full of gentle salutations—and soft responses—speaking—not like the trumpet stop of some ill-made organ, in which many an eye I talk to, holds coarse converse—but whispering soft—like the last low accent of an expiring saint—'How can you live comfortless, captain *Shandy*, and alone, without a bosom to lean your head on—or trust your cares to?'

It was an eye—

But I shall be in love with it myself, if I say another word about it.

—It did my uncle *Toby's* business.

Laurence Sterne (1713–1768)
The Life and Opinions of Tristram Shandy,
Book VIII, Chaps. 13, 14, 24, 25

LAND BEFORE LOOKS

Awa' wi' your witchcraft o' beauty's alarms,
The slender bit beauty you grasp in your arms!
O, gi'e me the lass that has acres o' charms,
O, gi'e me the lass wi' the weel-stockit farms.

Chorus:

Then hey for a lass wi' a tocher![1] then hey for a lass wi' a
tocher!
Then hey for a lass wi' a tocher! the nice yellow guineas
for me.

Your beauty's a flower in the morning that blows,
And withers the faster the faster it grows;
But the rapturous charm o' the bonnie green knowes,[2]
Ilk spring they're new deckit wi' bonnie white yowes.[3]
Then hey, etc.

And e'en when this beauty your bosom has blest,
The brightest o' beauty may cloy, when possest;
But the sweet yellow darlings wi' Geordie imprest,
The langer ye ha'e them, the mair they're carest.
Then hey, etc.

ROBERT BURNS (1759–1796)
Songs

[1] Dowry.   [2] Hillocks.   [3] Ewes.

LINKED BY POETRY

In 1844 Elizabeth Barrett published two volumes of collected poems. They contained a tribute to Robert Browning's poetry. The admiration was mutual. He wrote to her, interned as an invalid in her 'crypt' in Wimpole Street, and used the words 'I love you' to the woman whom he had never seen. She answered modestly as 'a devoted admirer of your works'. But soon they met, soon they married, and later, with the escape from her family and Wimpole Street, she sufficiently recovered her strength to be the mother of a son at the age of forty three. The union began with these letters.

Robert Browning to Elizabeth Barrett.

New Cross, Hatcham, Surrey
January 10th, 1845

I love your verses with all my heart, dear Miss Barrett— and this is no off-hand complimentary letter that I shall write, —whatever else, no prompt matter-of-course recognition of your genius, and there a graceful and natural end of the thing. Since the day last week when I first read your poems, I quite laugh to remember how I have been turning and turning again in my mind what I should be able to tell you of their effect upon me, for in the first flush of delight I thought I would this once get out of my habit of purely passive enjoyment, when I do really enjoy, and thoroughly justify my admiration— perhaps even, as a loyal fellow-craftsman should, try and find fault and do you some little good to be proud of hereafter!— but nothing comes of it all—so into me has it gone, and part of me has it become, this great living poetry of yours, not a flower of which but took root and grew—Oh, how different that is from lying to be dried and pressed flat, and prized highly, and put in a book with a proper account at top and bottom, and shut up and put away . . . and the book called a 'Flora', besides! After all, I need not give up the thought of doing that, too, in time; because even now, talking with who-ever is worthy, I can give a reason for my faith in one and another excellence, the fresh strange music, the affluent language, the exquisite pathos and true new brave thought; but in thus addressing myself to you—your own self, and for the first time, my feeling rises altogether. I do, as I say, love these books with all my heart—and I love you too. Do you know I was once not very far from seeing—really seeing you? Mr. Kenyon said to me one morning 'Would you like to see Miss Barrett?', then he went to announce me,—then he returned . . . you were too unwell, and now it is years ago, and I feel as at some untoward passage in my travels, as if I had been close, so close, to some world's-wonder in chapel or crypt, only a screen to push and I might have entered, but there was some slight, so it now seems, slight and just sufficient bar to admission, and the half-opened door shut, and I went home my thousands of miles, and the sight was never to be?

Well, these Poems were to be, and this true thankful joy and pride with which I feel myself,

Yours ever faithfully,

Robert Browning

HER REPLY

50 Wimpole Street
Jan. 11th, 1845

I thank you, dear Mr. Browning, from the bottom of my heart. You meant to give me pleasure by your letter—and even if the object had not been answered, I ought still to thank you. But it is thoroughly answered. Such a letter from such a hand! Sympathy is dear—very dear to me: but the sympathy of a poet, and of such a poet, is the quintessence of sympathy of me! Will you take back my gratitude for it?—agreeing, too, that of all the commerce done in the world, from Tyre to Carthage, the exchange of sympathy for gratitude is the most princely thing!

For the rest you draw me on with your kindness. It is difficult to get rid of people when you once have given them too much pleasure—*that* is a fact, and we will not stop for the moral of it. What I was going to say—after a little natural hesitation—is, that if ever you emerge without inconvenient effort from your 'passive state', and will *tell* me of such faults as rise to the surface and strike you as important in my poems (for of course, I do not think of troubling you with criticism in detail), you will confer a lasting obligation on me, and one which I shall value so much, that I covet it at a distance. I do not pretend to any extraordinary meekness under criticism and it is possible enough that I might not be altogether obedient to yours. But with my high respect for your power in your Art and for your experience as an artist, it would be quite impossible for me to hear a general observation of yours on what appear to you my master-faults, without being the better for it hereafter in some way. I ask for only a sentence or two of general observation—and I do not ask even for *that*, so as to tease you—but in the humble, low voice, which is so excellent a thing in women—particularly when they go a-begging! The most frequent general criticism I receive, is, I think, upon the style,—'if I *would* but change my style'! But *that* is an objection (isn't it?) to the writer bodily? Buffon says, and every sincere writer must feel, that 'Le style c'est l'homme'; a fact, however, scarcely calculated to lessen that objection with certain critics.

Is it indeed true that I was so near to the pleasure and honour of making your acquaintance and can it be true that you look back upon the lost opportunity with any regret? *But*—you know—if you had entered the 'crypt', you might have caught cold, or been tired to death, and *wished* yourself 'a thousand miles off'; which would have been worse than travelling them. It is not my interest, however, to put such thoughts in your head about its being 'all for the best'; and I would rather hope (as I do) that what I lost by one chance I may recover by some future one. Winters shut me up as they do dormouse's eyes; in the spring, *we shall see*: and I am so much better that I seem turning round to the outward world again. And in the meantime I have learnt to know your voice, not merely from the poetry but from the kindness in it. Mr. Kenyon often speaks of you—dear Mr. Kenyon!—who most unspeakably, or only speakably with tears in my eyes,—has been my friend and helper, and my book's friend and helper! critic and sympathizer, true friend of all hours! You know him well enough, I think, to understand that I must be grateful to him.

I am writing too much,—and notwithstanding that I am writing too much, I will write of one thing more. I will say that I am your debtor, not only for this cordial letter and for all the pleasure which came with it, but in other ways, and those the highest: and I will say that while I live to follow the divine art of poetry, in proportion to my love for it and my devotion to it, I must be a devout admirer and student of your works. This is in my heart to say to you—and I say it.

And for the rest, I am proud to remain,

Your obliged and faithful

Elizabeth B. Barrett

ROBERT BROWNING (1812–1889)
ELIZABETH BARRETT BROWNING (1806–1861)
Letters

'THE HEART'S A WONDER'

━━━━◦◦❁◦◦━━━━

In J. M. Synge's famous comedy 'The Playboy of the Western World', which caused an uproar at the Abbey Theatre, Dublin, because of its supposed libel on the Irish people, Christy Mahon, wandering into a shebeen in Mayo, is accepted as a wondrous hero because he claims to have killed his father in a fight. Here's a fellow indeed, think the villagers, including the romantically minded Pegeen, the inn-keeper's daughter. Christy woos her in the language of a poet. He is proved to be a liar in this matter of 'slaying his da' when the old man turns up and the two go off together. But Pegeen, though she must part with such a fraud, ends in lamentation, crying 'Oh my grief, I've lost him surely. I've lost the only Playboy of the Western World'. The reader or play-goer may fancy that he comes back to her after all and is accepted. But that is surmise; here is some of their grand talk of a marriage after Christy has proved himself a champion in the village sports and races.

Pegeen (*radiantly, wiping his face with her shawl*). Well, you're the lad, and you'll have great times from this out when you could win that wealth of prizes, and you sweating in the heat of noon!

Christy (*looking at her with delight*). I'll have great times if I win the crowning prize I'm seeking now, and that's your promise that you'll wed me in a fortnight, when our banns is called.

Pegeen (*backing away from him*). You've right daring to go ask me that, when all knows you'll be starting to some girl in your own townland, when your father's rotten in four months, or five.

Christy (*indignantly*). Starting from you, is it? (*He follows her.*) I will not, then, and when the airs is warming, in four months or five, it's then yourself and me should be pacing Neifin in the dews of night, the times sweet smells do be rising, and you'd see a little, shiny new moon, maybe, sinking on the hills.

Pegeen (*looking at him playfully*). And it's that kind of a poacher's love you'd make, Christy Mahon, on the sides of Neifin, when the night is down?

Christy. It's little you'll think if my love's a poacher's, or an earl's itself, when you'll feel my two hands stretched around you, and I squeezing kisses on your puckered lips, till I'd feel a kind of pity for the Lord God is all ages sitting lonesome in His golden chair.

Pegeen. That'll be right fun, Christy Mahon, and any girl would walk her heart out before she'd meet a young man was your like for eloquence, or talk at all.

Christy (encouraged). Let you wait, to hear me talking, till we're astray in Erris, when Good Friday's by, drinking a sup from a well, and making mighty kisses with our wetted mouths, or gaming in a gap of sunshine, with yourself stretched back unto your necklace, in the flowers of the earth.

Pegeen (in a low voice, moved by his tone). I'd be nice so, is it?

Christy (with rapture). If the mitred bishops seen you that time, they'd be the like of the holy prophets, I'm thinking, do be straining the bars of Paradise to lay eyes on the Lady Helen of Troy, and she abroad, pacing back and forward, with a nosegay in her golden shawl.

Pegeen (with real tenderness). And what is it I have, Christy Mahon, to make me fitting entertainment for the like of you, that has such poet's talking, and such bravery of heart.

Christy (in a low voice). Isn't there the light of seven heavens in your heart alone, the way you'll be an angel's lamp to me from this out, and I abroad in the darkness, spearing salmons in the Owen or the Carrowmore?

Pegeen. If I was your wife I'd be along with you those nights, Christy Mahon, the way you'd see I was a great hand at coaxing bailiffs, or coining funny nicknames for the stars of night.

Christy. You, is it? Taking your death in the hailstones, or in the fogs of dawn.

Pegeen. Yourself and me would shelter easy in a narrow bush; (*with a qualm of dread*) but we're only talking, maybe, for this would be a poor, thatched place to hold a fine lad is the like of you.

Christy (putting his arm round her). If I wasn't a good

Christian, it's on my naked knees I'd be saying my prayers and paters to every jackstraw you have roofing your head, and every stony pebble is paving the laneway to your door.

Pegeen (radiantly). If that's the truth I'll be burning candles from this out to the miracles of God that have brought you from the south to-day, and I with my gowns bought ready, the way that I can wed you, and not wait at all.

Christy. It's miracles, and that's the truth. Me there toiling a long while, and walking a long while, not knowing at all I was drawing all times nearer to this holy day.

Pegeen. And myself, a girl, was tempted often to go sailing the seas till I'd marry a Jew-man, with ten kegs of gold, and I not knowing at all there was the like of you drawing nearer, like the stars of God.

Christy. And to think I'm long years hearing women talking that talk, to all bloody fools, and this the first time I've heard the like of your voice talking sweetly for my own delight.

Pegeen. And to think it's me is talking sweetly, Christy Mahon, and I the fright of seven townlands for my biting tongue. Well, the heart's a wonder; and, I'm thinking, there won't be our like in Mayo, for gallant lovers, from this hour to-day. (*Drunken singing is heard outside.*) There's my father coming from the wake, and when he's had his sleep we'll tell him, for he's peaceful then.

J. M. SYNGE (1871–1909)
The Playboy of the Western World, Act III

COURTSHIP BETRAYED

In the Spring a fuller crimson comes upon the robin's breast;
In the Spring the wanton lapwing gets himself another crest;

In the Spring a livelier iris changes on the burnish'd dove;
In the Spring a young man's fancy lightly turns to thoughts of
    love.

Then her cheek was pale and thinner than should be for one so
    young,
And her eyes on all my motions with a mute observance hung.

And I said, 'My cousin Amy, speak, and speak the truth to me,
Trust me, cousin, all the current of my being sets to thee.'

On her pallid cheek and forehead came a colour and a light,
As I have seen the rosy red flushing in the northern light.

And she turn'd—her bosom shaken with a sudden storm of
    sighs—
All the spirit deeply dawning in the dark of hazel eyes—

Saying, 'I have hid my feelings, fearing they should do me
    wrong;'
Saying, 'Dost thou love me, cousin?' weeping, 'I have loved
    thee long'.

Love took up the glass of Time, and turn'd it in his glowing
    hands;
Every moment, lightly shaken, ran itself in golden sands.

Love took up the harp of Life, and smote on all the chords
    with might;
Smote the chord of Self, that, trembling, pass'd in music out
    of sight.

Many a morning on the moorland did we hear the copses ring,
And her whisper throng'd my pulses with the fulness of the
  Spring.

Many an evening by the waters did we watch the stately ships,
And our spirits rush'd together at the touching of the lips.

O my cousin, shallow-hearted! O my Amy, mine no more!
O the dreary, dreary moorland! O the barren, barren shore!

Falser than all fancy fathoms, falser than all songs have sung,
Puppet to a father's threat, and servile to a shrewish tongue!

Is it well to wish thee happy?—having known me—to decline
On a range of lower feelings and a narrower heart than mine!

Yet it shall be; thou shalt lower to this level day by day,
What is fine within thee growing coarse to sympathise with
  clay.

As the husband is, the wife is: thou art mated with a clown,
And the grossness of his nature will have weight to drag thee
down.

ALFRED, LORD TENNYSON (1809–1892)
Locksley Hall

VIRTUE AND VAPOURS

Dear Aunt,

I am much obliged to you for the kindness you intended me, in recommending Mr. Leadbeater to me for an husband: But I must be so free as to tell you, he is a man no-way suited to my inclination. I despise, 'tis true, the idle rants of Romance; but am inclinable to think there may be an extreme on the other side of the question.

The first time the *honest man* came to see me, in the way you were pleased to put into his head, was one Sunday after sermon-time.

I have heard, said he, a most excellent sermon just now: Dr. Thomas is a fine man truly: Did you ever hear him, madam? No, sir: I generally go to my own parish-church. That's right, madam, to be sure: What was your subject to-day? The Pharisee and the Publican, sir. A very good one truly; Dr. Thomas would have made fine work upon that subject. His text to-day was, Evil communications corrupt good manners. A good subject, sir; I doubt not the doctor made a fine discourse upon it. O, ay, madam, he can't make a bad one upon any subject. I run for the tea-kettle; for, thought I, we shall have all the heads of a sermon immediately.

At tea he gave me an account of all the Religious Societies, unask'd; and how many boys they had put out 'prentices, and girls they had taught to knit, and sing Psalms. To all which I gave a nod of approbation, and was just able to say (for I began to be horribly in the vapours), It was a very excellent charity. O, ay madam, said he again (for that's his word, I find), a very excellent one truly; it is snatching so many brands out of the fire. You are a contributor, sir, I doubt not. O, ay, madam, to be sure; every good man would contribute to such a worthy charity, to be sure. No doubt, sir, a blessing attends upon all who promote so worthy a design. O, ay, madam, no doubt, as you say: I am sure I have found it; blessed be God! And then he twang'd his nose, and lifted up his eyes, as if in an ejaculation.

O, my good Aunt, what a man is here for an husband! At last came the happy moment of his taking leave; for I would not ask him to stay supper: And moreover, he talk'd of going to a lecture at St. Helen's. And then (tho' I had an opportunity of saying little more than Yes, and No, all the time; for he took the vapours he had put me into, for devotion, or gravity at least, I believe) he press'd my hand, look'd *frightfully* kind, and gave me to understand as a mark of his favour, that if, upon further conversation, and inquiry into my character, he should happen to like me as well as he did from my behaviour and person; why, truly, I need not fear in time, being blessed with him for my husband!

This, my good Aunt, may be a mighty safe way of travelling toward the Land of Matrimony, as far as I know; but I cannot help wishing for a little more *entertainment* on our *journey*. I am willing to believe Mr. Leadbeater an honest man, but am, at the same time, afraid his religious turn of temper, however in itself commendable, would better suit with a woman who centres all desert in a *solemn appearance*, than with, dear aunt,
                    Your greatly obliged Kinswoman.

SAMUEL RICHARDSON (1689–1761)
Familiar Letters on Important Occasions

D

UNIVERSAL UNION

The fountains mingle with the river
And the rivers with the ocean,
The winds of heaven mix for ever
With a sweet emotion;
Nothing in the world is single,
All things by a law divine
In another's being mingle—
Why not I with thine?

See the mountains kiss high heaven,
And the waves clasp one another;
No sister-flower would be forgiven
If it disdain'd its brother;
And the sunlight clasps the earth,
And the moonbeams kiss the sea—
What are all these kissings worth,
If thou kiss not me?

P. B. SHELLEY (1792–1822)
Collected Poems

QUIET WORDS IN A STORM

———————— ⤛⤜⟡⤝⤞ ————————

George Meredith's brilliant Irish woman Diana Meryon, of the epigrams
as well as the Crossways, had bitter experience of men before she accepted her
steady, tongue-tied, long-adoring Mr. Redworth. After stormy years she walks
with him among the woods, gale-tossed but at peace. Emma, eager for the match,
is Diana's admiring guardian, hostess, and devoted friend, Lady Dunstane.

Meanwhile the feet of the couple were going faster than their
heads to the end of the journey. Diana knew she would have
to hoist the signal—and how? The prospect was dumbfounder-
ing. She had to think of appeasing her Emma. Redworth, for
his part, actually supposed she had accepted his escorting in
proof of the plain friendship offered him over-night.

'What do your "birds" do in weather like this?' she said.

'Cling to their perches and wait patiently. It's the bad
time with them when you don't hear them chirp.'

'Of course you foretold the gale.'

'Oh, well, it did not require a shepherd or a skipper for
that.'

'Your grand gift will be useful to a yachtsman.'

'You like yachting. When I have tried my new schooner in
the Channel, she is at your command for as long as you and
Lady Dunstane please.'

'So you acknowledge that birds—things of nature—have
their bad time?'

'They profit ultimately by the deluge and the wreck.
Nothing on earth is "tucked-up" in perpetuity.'

'Except the dead. But why should the schooner be at our
command?'

'I shall be in Ireland.'

He could not have said sweeter to her ears or more touching.

'We shall hardly feel safe without the weatherwise on board.'

'You may count on my man Barnes; I have proved him. He
is up to his work even when he's bilious: only, in that case,

occurring about once a fortnight, you must leave him to fight
it out with the elements.'

'I rather like men of action to have a temper.'

'I can't say much for a bilious temper.'

The weather to-day really seemed of that kind, she remarked.
He assented, in the shrug manner—not to dissent; she might
say what she would. He helped nowhere to a lead; and so
quick are the changes of mood at such moments that she was
now far from him under the failure of an effort to come near.
But thoughts of Emma pressed.

'The name of the new schooner? Her name is her picture to
me.'

'I wanted you to christen her.'

'Launched without a name?'

'I took a liberty.'

Needless to ask, but she did. 'With whom?'

'I named her Diana.'

'May the Goddess of the silver bow and crescent protect
her! To me the name is ominous of mischance.'

'I would commit my fortunes and life!' . . . He checked his
tongue, ejaculating: 'Omens!'

She had veered straight away from her romantic aspirations
to the blunt extreme of thinking that a widow should be
wooed in unornamented matter-of-fact, as she is wedded,
with a 'wilt thou', and 'I will', and no decorative illusions.
Downright, for the unpoetic creature, if you please! So she
rejected the accompaniment of the silver Goddess and high
seas for an introduction of the crisis.

'This would be a thunderer on our coasts. I had a trial of
my sailing powers in the Mediterranean.'

As she said it, her musings on him then, with the contrast
of her position toward him now, fierily brushed her cheeks;
and she wished him the man to make one snatch at her poor
lost small butterfly bit of freedom, so that she might suddenly
feel in haven, at peace with her expectant Emma. He could
have seen the inviting consciousness, but he was absurdly
watchful lest the flying sprays of border trees should strike

her. He mentioned his fear, and it became an excuse for her seeking protection of her veil. 'It is our natural guardian,' she said.

'Not much against timber,' said he.

The worthy creature's anxiety was of the pattern of cavaliers escorting dames—an exaggeration of honest zeal; a present example of clownish goodness, it might seem; until entering the larch and firwood along the beaten heights, there was a rocking and straining of the shallow-rooted trees in a tremendous gust that quite pardoned him for curving his arm in a hoop about her and holding a shoulder in front. The veil did her positive service.

He was honourably scrupulous not to presume. A right good unimpulsive gentleman: the same that she had always taken him for and liked.

'These firs are not taproots,' he observed, by way of apology.

Her dress volumed and her ribands rattled and chirruped on the verge of the slope. 'I will take your arm here,' she said.

Redworth received the little hand, saying: 'Lean to me.'

They descended upon great surges of wind piping and driving every light surface-atom as foam; and they blinked and shook; even the man was shaken. But their arms were interlinked and they grappled; the battering enemy made them one. It might mean nothing, or everything: to him it meant the sheer blissful instant.

At the foot of the hill, he said: 'It's harder to keep to the terms of yesterday.'

'What were they?' she said, and took his breath more than the fury of the storm had done.

'Raise the veil, I beg.'

'Widows do not wear it.'

The look revealed to him was a fugitive of the wilds, no longer the glittering shooter of arrows.

'Have you? . . .' changed to me, was the signification understood. 'Can you?—for life! Do you think you can?'

His poverty in the pleading language melted her. 'What I cannot do, my best of friends, is to submit to be seated on a throne, with you petitioning. Yes, as far as concerns this hand of mine, if you hold it worthy of you. We will speak of that. Now tell me the name of the weed trailing along the hedge there.'

He knew it well; a common hedgerow weed; but the placid diversion baffled him. It was clematis, he said.

'It drags in the dust when it has no firm arm to cling to. I passed it beside you yesterday with a flaunting mind and not a suspicion of a likeness. How foolish I was! I could volubly sermonize; only it should be a young maid to listen. Forgive me the yesterday.'

'You have never to ask. You withdraw your hand—was I rough?'

'No,' she smiled demurely; 'it must get used to the shackles: but my cottage is in sight. I have a growing love for the place. We will enter it like plain people—if you think of coming in.'

As she said it she had a slight shock of cowering under eyes tolerably hawkish in their male glitter; but her coolness was not disturbed, and without any apprehensions she reflected on what has been written of the silly division and war of the sexes:—which two might surely enter on an engagement to live together amiably, unvexed by that barbarous old fowl and falcon interlude. Cool herself, she imagined the same of him, having good grounds for the delusion; so they passed through the cottage-garden and beneath the low porchway, into her little sitting-room, where she was proceeding to speak composedly of her preference for cottages while untying her bonnet strings:—'If I had begun my life in a cottage!'—when really a big storm-wave caught her from shore and swirled her to mid-sea, out of every sensibility but the swimming one of her loss of self in the man.

'You would not have been here!' was all he said. She was up at his heart, fast-locked, undergoing a change greater than the sea works; her thoughts one blush, her brain a fire-fount. This was not like being seated on a throne.

'There,' said he, loosening his hug, 'now you belong to me! I know you from head to foot. After that, my darling, I

could leave you for years, and call you wife, and be sure of you.
I could swear it for you—my life on it! That's what I think of
you. Don't wonder that I took my chance—the first;—I have
waited!'

Truer word was never uttered, she owned, coming into
some harmony with man's kiss on her mouth: the man
violently metamorphozed to a stranger, acting on rights she
had given him. And who was she to dream of denying them?
Not an idea in her head! Bound verily to be thankful for such
love, on hearing that it dated from the night in Ireland. . . .
'So in love with you that, on my soul, your happiness was my
marrow—whatever you wished; anything you chose. It's
reckoned a fool's part. No, it's love: the love of a woman—
the one woman! I was like the hand of a clock to the springs.
I taught this old watch-dog of a heart to keep guard and bury
the bones you tossed him.'

GEORGE MEREDITH (1828–1909)
Diana of the Crossways, Chap. 43

PRIDE PUT IN ITS PLACE

Silvius.   O dear Phebe,
If ever—as that ever may be near—
You meet in some fresh cheek the power of fancy,
Then shall you know the wounds invisible
That love's keen arrows make.

Phebe.   But, till that time,
Come not thou near me: and, when that time comes,
Afflict me with thy mocks, pity me not;
As, till that time, I shall not pity thee.

Rosalind (coming forward). And why, I pray you? Who might
    be your mother,
That you insult, exult, and all at once,
Over the wretched? What though you have no beauty,—
As, by my faith, I see no more in you
Than without candle may go dark to bed,—
Must you be therefore proud and pitiless?
Why, what means this? Why do you look on me?
I see no more in you than in the ordinary
Of nature's sale-work:—'Od's my little life,
I think she means to tangle my eyes too!—
No, faith, proud mistress, hope not after it:
'Tis not your inky brows, your black-silk hair,
Your bugle eyeballs, nor your cheek of cream,
That can entame my spirits to your worship.—
You foolish shepherd, wherefore do you follow her,
Like foggy south, puffing with wind and rain?
You are a thousand times a properer man
Than she a woman: 'tis such fools as you
That makes the world full of ill-favour'd children:
'Tis not her glass, but you, that flatters her;
And out of you she sees herself more proper
Than any of her lineaments can show her.—

But, mistress, know yourself: down on your knees,
And thank heaven, fasting, for a good man's love:
For I must tell you friendly in your ear,—
Sell when you can: you are not for all markets:
Cry the man mercy; love him; take his offer.

WILLIAM SHAKESPEARE (1564–1616)
As You Like It, Act III, Scene 5

HAMPSTEAD LOVERS

This is the last but one of the surviving letters of John Keats to Fanny Brawne, the young neighbour in Hampstead whom he courted with a feverish urgency despite the opposition of his friends, here dismissed as a 'coterie' of 'tattlers and inquisitors'. Had they wedded, 'a marriage of true minds' was not to be expected, and Keats knew that a wedding was unlikely, since when this letter was written in July, 1820, his life was a slender thread. 'The hectic', of tuberculosis as well as of devotion to Fanny, was raging in his blood. He left England for the sunshine of Italy two months later and in five months he was dead.

My dearest Fanny,

My head is puzzled this morning, and I scarce know what I shall say though I am full of a hundred things. 'Tis certain I would rather be writing to you this morning, notwithstanding the alloy of grief in such an occupation, than enjoy any other pleasure, with health to boot, un-connected with you. Upon my soul I have loved you to the extreme. I wish you could know the Tenderness with which I continually brood over your different aspects of countenance, action and dress. I see you come down in the morning: I see you meet me at the Window —I see every thing over again eternally that I ever have seen. If I get on the pleasant clue I live in a sort of happy misery, if on the unpleasant 'tis miserable misery. You complain of my illtreating you in word thought and deed—I am sorry,— at times I feel bitterly sorry that I ever made you unhappy— my excuse is that those words have been wrung from me by the sharpness of my feelings. At all events and in any case I have been wrong; could I believe that I did it without any cause, I should be the most sincere of Penitents. I could give way to my repentant feelings now, I could recant all my suspicions, I could mingle with you heart and Soul though absent, were it not for some parts of your Letters. Do you suppose it possible I could ever leave you? You know what I think of myself and what of you. You know that I should feel how much it was my loss and how little yours. My friends laugh at you! I know some of them—when I know them all I shall never think of them again as friends or even acquaintance.

My friends have behaved well to me in every instance but one, and there they have become tattlers, and inquisitors into my conduct: spying upon a secret I would rather die than share it with any body's confidence. For this I cannot wish them well, I care not to see any of them again. If I am the Theme, I will not be the Friend of idle Gossips. Good gods what a shame it is our Loves should be so put into the microscope of a Coterie. Their laughs should not affect you (I may perhaps give you reasons some day for these laughs, for I suspect a few people to hate me well enough, for reasons I know of, who have pretended a great friendship for me) when in competition with one, who if he never should see you again would make you the Saint of his memory. These Laughers, who do not like you, who envy you for your Beauty, who would have God-bless'd me from you for ever: who were plying me with disencouragements with respect to you eternally. People are revengeful—do not mind them—do nothing but love me—if I knew that for certain life and health will in such event be a heaven, and death itself will be less painful. I long to believe in immortality. I shall never be able to bid you an entire farewell. If I am destined to be happy with you here— how short is the longest Life. I wish to believe in immortality —I wish to live with you for ever. Do not let my name ever pass between you and those laughers, if I have no other merit than the great Love for you, that were sufficient to keep me sacred and unmentioned in such Society.

If I have been cruel and unjust I swear my love has ever been greater than my cruelty which lasts but a minute whereas my Love come what will shall last for ever. If concession to me has hurt your Pride, god knows I have had little pride in my heart when thinking of you. Your name never passes my Lips—do not let mine pass yours—Those People do not like me. After reading my Letter you even then wish to see me. I am strong enough to walk over—but I dare not. I shall feel so much pain in parting with you again. My dearest love, I am affraid to see you, I am strong but not strong enough to see you. Will my arm be ever round you again? And if so shall I be obliged to leave you again? My sweet Love! I am happy whilst I believe your first Letter. Let me be but certain that you are mine heart and soul, and I could die more happily than I could otherwise live. If you think me cruel—if you think I have sleighted you—do muse it over again, and see into my heart. My Love to you is 'true as truth's simplicity and simpler than the infancy of truth' as I think I once said before. How could I slight you? How threaten to leave you? not in the spirit of a Threat to you—no—but in the spirit of Wretchedness in myself. My fairest, my delicious, my angel Fanny! do not believe me such a vulgar fellow. I will be as patient in illness and as believing in Love as I am able.

Yours for ever my dearest

John Keats

JOHN KEATS (1795–1821)
Letters

TEARS WATER THE MILK

I am a broken-hearted milkman, in grief I'm arrayed,
Through keeping of the company of a young servant maid,
Who lived on board and wages the house to keep clean
In a gentleman's family near Paddington Green.

Chorus:

    She was as beautiful as a butterfly
    And as a proud as a Queen
    Was pretty little Polly Perkins of
    Paddington Green.

She'd an ankle like an antelope and a step like a deer,
A voice like a blackbird, so mellow and clear,
Her hair hung in ringlets so beautiful and long,
I thought that she loved me but I found I was wrong.

When I'd rattle in a morning and cry 'milk below',
At the sound of my milk-cans her face she would show
With a smile upon her countenance and a laugh in her eye,
If I thought she'd have loved me, I'd have laid down to die.

When I asked her to marry me she said 'Oh! what stuff',
And told me to 'drop it, for she had quite enough
Of my nonsense'—at the same time I'd been very kind,
But to marry a milkman she didn't feel inclined.

Oh, the man that has me must have silver and gold,
A chariot to ride in and be handsome and bold,
His hair must be curly as any watch spring,
And his whiskers as big as a brush for clothing.

The words that she uttered went straight through my heart,
I sobbed and I sighed, and straight did depart;
With a tear on my eyelid as big as a bean,
Bidding good-bye to Polly and Paddington Green.

In six months she married,—this hard-hearted girl,—
But it was not a Wi-count, and it was not a Nearl,
It was not a 'Baronite', but a shade or two wuss,
It was a bow-legged conductor of a twopenny bus.

ANON
(nineteenth century)

LOVE, CARDS, AND MEDICINE

Lady Dorothy Osborne married Sir William Temple, the diplomatist, in 1655. They had been compelled by separations caused by his career to tell their love in letters, in the writing of which both excelled.

To Sir William Temple

(1653)

Sir, Your last letter came like a pardon to one upon the block. I had given over the hopes on't, having received my letters by the other carrier, who was always wont to be last. The loss put me hugely out of order, and you would have both pitied and laughed at me if you could have seen how woodenly I entertained the widow, who came hither the day before, and surprised me very much. Not being able to say anything, I got her to cards, and there with a great deal of patience lost my money to her;—or rather I gave it as my ransom. In the midst of our play, in comes my blessed boy with your letter, and, in earnest, I was not able to disguise the joy it gave me, though one was by that is not much your friend, and took notice of a blush that for my life I could not keep back. I put up the letter in my pocket, and made what haste I could to lose the money I had left, that I might take occasion to go fetch some more; but I did not make such haste back again, I can assure you. I took time enough to have coined myself some money if I had had the art on't, and left my brother enough to make all his addresses to her if he were so disposed. I know not whether he was pleased or not, but I am sure I was.

You make so reasonable demands that 'tis not fit you should be denied. You ask my thoughts but at one hour; you will think me bountiful, I hope, when I shall tell you that I know no hour when you have them not. No, in earnest, my very dreams are yours, and I have got such a habit of thinking of you that any other thought intrudes and proves uneasy to me.

I drink your health every morning in a drench that would poison a horse I believe, and 'tis the only way I have to persuade myself to take it. 'Tis the infusion of steel, and makes me so horribly sick, that every day at ten o'clock I am making my will and taking leave of all my friends. You will believe you are not forgot then. They tell me I must take this ugly drink a fortnight, and then begin another as bad; but unless you say so too, I do not think I shall. 'Tis worse than dying by the half.

*

Sir William wrote back later from Ireland,

I know you love me still; you promised me, and that's all the security I can have in this world. 'Tis that which makes all things else seem nothing to it, so high it sets me; and so high, indeed, that should I ever fall 'twould dash me all to pieces. Methinks your very charity should make you love me more now than ever, by seeing me so much more unhappy than I used, by being so much farther from you, for that is all the measure can be taken of my good or ill condition. Justice, I am sure, will oblige you to it, since you have no other means left in the world of rewarding such a passion as mine, which, sure, is of a much richer value than anything in the world besides. Should you save my life again, should you make me absolute master of your fortune and your person too, I should accept none of this in any part of payment, but look upon you as one behindhand with me still. 'Tis no vanity this, but a true sense of how pure and how refined a nature my passion is, which none can ever know except my own heart, unless you find it out by being there.

How hard it is to think of ending when I am writing to you; but it must be so, and I must ever be subject to other people's occasions, and so never, I think, master of my own. This is too true, both in respect of this fellow's post that is bawling at me for my letter, and of my father's delays. They kill me; but patience,—would anybody but I were here. Yet you may command me ever at one minute's warning. Had I not heard from you by this last, in earnest I had resolved to have gone with this, and given my father the slip for all his caution. He tells me still of a little time; but, alas! who knows not what mischances and how great changes have often happened in a little time?

For God's sake let me hear of all your motions, when and where I may hope to see you. Let us hope this cloud, this absence that has overcast all my contentment, may pass away, and I am confident there's a clear sky attends us. My dearest dear, adieu.

LADY DOROTHY OSBORNE (1627–1695)
SIR WILLIAM TEMPLE (1628–1699)
Letters

LOVE IS LIKE A DIZZINESS

I lately lived in quiet case
    An' never wish'd to marry, O!
But when I saw my Peggy's face,
    I felt a sad quandary, O!
Though wild as ony Athol deer,
    She has trepann'd me fairly, O!
Her cherry cheeks an' een sae clear
    Torment me late an early, O!
      O, love, love, love!
        Love is like a dizziness;
        It winna let a poor body
        Gang about his biziness!

To tell my feats this single week
    Wad mak a daft-like diary, O!
I drave my cart outow'r a dike,
    My horses in a miry, O!
I wear my stockings white an' blue,
    My love's sae fierce an' fiery, O!
I drill the land that I should plough,
    An' plough the drills entirely, O!
      O, love, love, love! etc.

Her wily glance I'll ne'er forget,
    The dear, the lovely blinkin o't
Has pierced me through an' through the heart,
    An' plagues me wi' the prinking o't.
I tried to sing, I tried to pray,
    I tried to drown't wi' drinkin' o't,
I tried wi' sport to drive't away,
    But ne'er can sleep for thinkin' o't.
      O, love, love, love! etc.

Nae man can tell what pains I prove,
 Or how severe my pliskie,[1] O!
I swear I'm sairer drunk wi' love
 Than ever I was wi' whisky, O!
For love has raked me fore an' aft,
 I scarce can lift a leggie, O!
I first grew dizzy, then gaed daft,
 An soon I'll dee for Peggy, O!
  O, love, love, love!
   Love is like a dizziness
   It winna let a poor body
   Gang about his biziness!

JAMES HOGG (1776–1835)
Songs

[1] Plight.

COURTSHIP AND QUESTIONNAIRE

—◦◦≈∧∧∧≈◦◦—

(Jack Worthing and the Hon. Gwendolen Fairfax.)

Jack. Well . . . may I propose to you now?

Gwendolen. I think it would be an admirable opportunity. And to spare you any possible disappointment, Mr. Worthing, I think it only fair to tell you quite frankly beforehand that I am fully determined to accept you.

Jack. Gwendolen!

Gwendolen. Yes, Mr. Worthing, what have you got to say to me?

Jack. You know what I have got to say to you.

Gwendolen. Yes, but you don't say it.

Jack. Gwendolen, will you marry me? (*Goes on his knees.*)

Gwendolen. Of course I will, darling. How long you have been about it! I am afraid you have had very little experience in how to propose.

Jack. My own one, I have never loved any one in the world but you.

Gwendolen. Yes, but men often propose for practice. I know my brother Gerald does. All my girl-friends tell me so. What wonderfully blue eyes you have, Ernest! They are quite, quite blue. I hope you will always look at me just like that, especially when there are other people present.

Enter Lady Bracknell.

Lady Bracknell. Mr. Worthing! Rise, sir, from this semi-recumbent posture. It is most indecorous.

Gwendolen. Mamma! (*He tries to rise; she restrains him.*) I must beg you to retire. This is no place for you. Besides, Mr. Worthing has not quite finished yet.

Lady Bracknell. Finished, what, may I ask?

Gwendolen. I am engaged to Mr. Worthing, mamma. (*They rise together.*)

Lady Bracknell. Pardon me, you are not engaged to any one. When you do become engaged to some one, I, or your father, should his health permit him, will inform you of the fact. An engagement should come on a young girl as a surprise, pleasant or unpleasant, as the case may be. It is hardly a matter that she could be allowed to arrange for herself. . . . And now I have a few questions to put to you, Mr. Worthing. While I am making these inquiries, you, Gwendolen, will wait for me below in the carriage.

Gwendolen (reproachfully). Mamma!

Lady Bracknell. In the carriage, Gwendolen! (*Gwendolen goes to the door. She and Jack blow kisses to each other behind Lady Bracknell's back. Lady Bracknell looks vaguely about as if she could not understand what the noise was. Finally she turns round.*) Gwendolen, the carriage.

Gwendolen. Yes, mamma. (*Goes out, looking back at Jack.*)

Lady Bracknell (sitting down). You can take a seat, Mr. Worthing. (*Looks in her pocket for note-book and pencil.*)

Jack. Thank you, Lady Bracknell, I prefer standing.

Lady Bracknell (pencil and note-book in hand). I feel bound to tell you that you are not down on my list of eligible young men, although I have the same list as the dear Duchess of Bolton has. We work together, in fact. However, I am quite ready to enter your name, should your answers be what a really affectionate mother requires. Do you smoke?

Jack. Well, yes, I must admit I smoke.

Lady Bracknell. I am glad to hear it. A man should always have an occupation of some kind. There are far too many idle men in London as it is. How old are you?

Jack. Twenty-nine.

Lady Bracknell. A very good age to be married at. I have always been of opinion that a man who desires to get married should know either everything or nothing. Which do you know?

Jack (after some hesitation). I know nothing, Lady Bracknell.

Lady Bracknell. I am pleased to hear it. I do not approve of anything that tampers with natural ignorance. Ignorance is like a delicate exotic fruit; touch it, and the bloom is gone. The whole theory of modern education is radically unsound. Fortunately in England, at any rate, education produces no effect whatsoever. If it did, it would prove a serious danger to the upper classes, and probably lead to acts of violence in Grosvenor Square. What is your income?

Jack. Between seven and eight thousand a year.

Lady Bracknell (makes a note in her book). In land, or in investments?

Jack. In investments, chiefly.

Lady Bracknell. That is satisfactory. What between the duties expected of one during one's lifetime, and the duties exacted from one after one's death, land has ceased to be either a profit or a pleasure. It gives one position, and prevents one from keeping it up. That's all that can be said about land.

Jack. I have a country house with some land, of course, attached to it, about fifteen hundred acres, I believe; but I don't depend on that for my real income. In fact, as far as I can make out, the poachers are the only people who make anything out of it.

Lady Bracknell. A country house! How many bedrooms? Well, that point can be cleared up afterwards. You have a town house, I hope? A girl with a simple, unspoiled nature, like Gwendolen, could hardly be expected to reside in the country.

Jack. Well, I own a house in Belgrave Square, but it is let by the year to Lady Bloxham. Of course, I can get it back whenever I like, at six month's notice.

Lady Bracknell. Lady Bloxham? I don't know her.

Jack. Oh, she goes about very little. She is a lady considerably advanced in years.

Lady Bracknell. Ah, nowadays that is no guarantee of respectability of character. What number in Belgrave Square.

Jack. 149.

Lady Bracknell (shaking her head). The unfashionable side. I thought there was something. However, that could easily be altered.

Jack. Do you mean the fashion, or the side?

Lady Bracknell (*sternly*). Both, if necessary, I presume. What are your politics?

Jack. Well, I am afraid I really have none. I am a Liberal Unionist.

Lady Bracknell. Oh, they count as Tories. They dine with us. Or come in the evening, at any rate. Now to minor matters. Are your parents living?

Jack. I have lost both my parents.

Lady Bracknell. To lose one parent, Mr. Worthing, may be regarded as a misfortune; to lose both looks like carelessness. Who was your father? He was evidently a man of some wealth. Was he born in what the Radical papers call the purple of commerce, or did he rise from the ranks of the aristocracy?

Jack. I am afraid I really don't know. The fact is, Lady Bracknell, I said I had lost my parents. It would be nearer the truth to say that my parents seem to have lost me. . . . I don't actually know who I am by birth. I was . . . well, I was found.

Lady Bracknell. Found!

Jack. The late Mr. Thomas Cardew, an old gentleman of a very charitable and kindly disposition, found me, and gave me the name of Worthing, because he happened to have a first-class ticket for Worthing in his pocket at the time. Worthing is a place in Sussex. It is a seaside resort.

Lady Bracknell. Where did the charitable gentleman who had a first-class ticket for this seaside resort find you?

Jack (*gravely*). In a hand-bag.

Lady Bracknell. A hand-bag?

Jack (*very seriously*). Yes, Lady Bracknell. I was in a hand-bag—a somewhat large, black leather hand-bag, with handles to it—an ordinary hand-bag in fact.

Lady Bracknell. In what locality did this Mr. James, or Thomas Cardew come across this ordinary hand-bag?

Jack. In the cloak-room at Victoria Station. It was given to him in mistake for his own.

Lady Bracknell. The cloak-room at Victoria Station?

Jack. Yes. The Brighton Line.

Lady Bracknell. The line is immaterial. Mr. Worthing, I confess I feel somewhat bewildered by what you have just told me. To be born, or at any rate bred, in a hand-bag, whether it had handles or not, seems to me to display a contempt for the ordinary decencies of family life that reminds one of the worst excesses of the French Revolution. And I presume you know what that unfortunate movement led to?

OSCAR WILDE (1856–1900)
The Importance of Being Earnest, Act I

SALLY IN OUR ALLEY

Of all the girls that are so smart
   There's none like pretty Sally;
She is the darling of my heart,
   And she lives in our alley.
There is no lady in the land
   Is half so sweet as Sally;
She is the darling of my heart,
   And she lives in our alley.

Her father he makes cabbage-nets
   And through the streets does cry 'em;
Her mother she sells laces long
   To such as please to buy 'em:
But sure such folks could ne'er beget
   So sweet a girl as Sally!
She is the darling of my heart,
   And she lives in our alley.

When she is by, I leave my work,
   I love her so sincerely;
My master comes like any Turk,
   And bangs me most severely—
But let him bang his bellyful,
   I'll bear it all for Sally;
She is the darling of my heart,
   And she lives in our alley.

Of all the days that's in the week
   I dearly love but one day—
And that's the day that comes betwixt
   A Saturday and Monday;

For then I'm drest all in my best
　To walk abroad with Sally;
She is the darling of my heart,
　And she lives in our alley.

My master carries me to church,
　And often am I blamed
Because I leave him in the lurch
　As soon as text is named;
I leave the church in sermon-time
　And slink away to Sally;
She is the darling of my heart,
　And she lives in our alley.

When Christmas comes about again
　O then I shall have money;
I'll hoard it up, and box it all,
　I'll give it to my honey;
I would it were ten thousand pound,
　I'd give it all to Sally;
She is the darling of my heart,
　And she lives in our alley.

My master and the neighbours all
　Make game of me and Sally,
And, but for her, I'd better be
　A slave and row a galley;
But when my seven long years are out
　O then I'll marry Sally,—
O then we'll wed, and then we'll bed . . .
　But not in our alley.

H. CAREY
Songs (eighteenth century)

PART TWO

THE WEDDING DAY

AT THE WEDDING MARCH

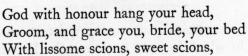

God with honour hang your head,
Groom, and grace you, bride, your bed
With lissome scions, sweet scions,
Out of hallowed bodies bred.

Each be other's comfort kind:
Déep, déeper than divined,
Divine charity, dear charity,
Fast you ever, fast bind.

Then let the march tread our ears:
I to him turn with tears
Who to wedlock, his wonder wedlock,
Deals triumph and immortal years.

GERARD MANLEY HOPKINS
(1844–1889)

FLORENCE DOMBEY AND THE DUST

They take the streets that are the quietest, and do not go near that in which her old home stands. It is a fair, warm summer morning, and the sun shines on them, as they walk towards the darkening mist that overspreads the City. Riches are uncovering in shops; jewels, gold, and silver flash in the goldsmith's sunny windows; and great houses cast a stately shade upon them as they pass. But through the light, and through the shade, they go on lovingly together, lost to everything around; thinking of no other riches, and no prouder home, than they have now in one another.

Gradually they come into the darker, narrower streets, where the sun, now yellow, and now red, is seen through the mist, only at street corners, and in small open spaces where there is a tree, or one of the innumerable churches, or a paved way and a flight of steps, or a curious little patch of garden, or a burying-ground, where the few tombs and tomb-stones are almost black. Lovingly and trustfully, through all the narrow yards and alleys and the shady streets, Florence goes, clinging to his arm, to be his wife.

Her heart beats quicker now, for Walter tells her that their church is very near. They pass a few great stacks of warehouses, with waggons at the doors, and busy carmen stopping up the way—but Florence does not see or hear them—and then the air is quiet, and the day is darkened, and she is trembling in a church which has a strange smell like a cellar.

The shabby little old man, ringer of the disappointed bell, is standing in the porch, and has put his hat in the font—for he is quite at home there, being sexton. He ushers them into an old brown, panelled, dusty vestry, like a corner-cupboard with the shelves taken out; where the wormy registers diffuse a smell like faded snuff, which has set the tearful Nipper sneezing.

Youthful, and how beautiful, the young bride looks, in this old dusty place, with no kindred object near her but her husband. There is a dusty old clerk, who keeps a sort of evaporated news shop underneath an archway opposite, behind a perfect fortification of posts. There is a dusty old pew-opener who only keeps herself, and finds that quite enough to do. There is a dusty old beadle (these are Mr. Toots's beadle and pew-opener of last Sunday), who has something to do with a Worshipful Company who have got a Hall in the next yard, with a stained-glass window in it that no mortal ever saw. There are dusty wooden ledges and cornices poked in and out over the altar, and over the screen and round the gallery, and over the inscription about what the Master and Wardens of the Worshipful Company did in one thousand six hundred and ninety-four. There are dusty old sounding-boards over the pulpit and reading-desk, looking like lids to be let down on the officiating ministers, in case of their giving offence. There is every possible provision for the accommodation of dust, except in the church-yard, where the facilities in that respect are very limited.

The Captain, Uncle Sol, and Mr. Toots are come; the clergyman is putting on his surplice in the vestry, while the clerk walks round him, blowing the dust off it; and the bride and bridegroom stand before the altar. There is no bridesmaid, unless Susan Nipper is one; and no better father than Captain Cuttle. A man with a wooden leg, chewing a faint apple and carrying a blue bag in his hand, looks in to see what is going on; but finding it nothing entertaining, stumps off again, and pegs his way among the echoes out of doors.

No gracious ray of light is seen to fall on Florence, kneeling at the altar with her timid head bowed down. The morning luminary is built out, and don't shine there. There is a meagre tree outside, where the sparrows are chirping a little; and there is a blackbird in an eyelet-hole of sun in a dyer's garret, over against the window, who whistles loudly whilst the service is performing; and there is the man with the wooden leg stumping away. The amens of the dusty clerk appear, like Macbeth's, to stick in his throat a little; but Captain Cuttle helps him out, and does it with so much goodwill that he interpolates three entirely new responses of that word, never introduced into the service before.

They are married, and have signed their names in one of the old sneezy registers, and the clergyman's surplice is restored to the dust, and the clergyman is gone home. In a dark corner of the dark church, Florence has turned to Susan Nipper, and is weeping in her arms. Mr. Toots's eyes are red. The Captain lubricates his nose. Uncle Sol has pulled down his spectacles from his forehead, and walked out to the door.

'God bless you, Susan; dearest Susan! If you ever can bear witness to the love I have for Walter, and the reason that I have to love him, do it for his sake. Good-bye! Good-bye!'

They have thought it better not to go back to the Midshipman, but to part so; a coach is waiting for them, near at hand.

Miss Nipper cannot speak; she only sobs and chokes, and hugs her mistress. Mr. Toots advances, urges her to cheer up, and takes charge of her. Florence gives him her hand—gives him, in the fulness of her heart, her lips—kisses Uncle Sol, and Captain Cuttle, and is borne away by her young husband.

But Susan cannot bear that Florence should go away with a mournful recollection of her. She had meant to be so different, that she reproaches herself bitterly. Intent on making one last effort to redeem her character, she breaks from Mr. Toots and runs away to find the coach, and show a parting smile. The Captain, divining her object, sets off after her; for he feels it his duty also to dismiss them with a cheer, if possible. Uncle Sol and Mr. Toots are left behind together, outside the church, to wait for them.

The coach is gone, but the street is steep, and narrow, and blocked up, and Susan can see it at a stand-still in the distance, she is sure. Captain Cuttle follows her as she flies down the hill, and waves his glazed hat as a general signal, which may attract the right coach and which may not.

Susan outstrips the Captain, and comes up with it. She looks in at the window, sees Walter, with the gentle face beside him, and claps her hands and screams:

'Miss Floy, my darling! look at me! We are all so happy now, dear! One more good-bye, my precious, one more!'

How Susan does it, she don't know, but she reaches to the window, kisses her, and has her arms about her neck, in a moment.

'We are all so—so happy now, my dear Miss Floy!' says Susan, with a suspicious catching in her breath. 'You, you won't be angry with me now. Now *will* you?'

'Angry, Susan!'

'No, no; I am sure you won't. I say you won't my pet, my dearest!' exclaims Susan; ' and here's the Captain too—your friend the Captain, you know—to say good-bye once more!'

'Hooroar, my Heart's Delight!' vociferates the Captain, with a countenance of strong emotion. 'Hooroar, Wal'r my lad. Hooroar! Hooroar!'

What with the young husband at one window, and the young wife at the other; the Captain hanging on at this door, and Susan Nipper holding fast by that; the coach obliged to go on whether it will or no, and all the other carts and coaches turbulent because it hesitates; there never was so much confusion on four wheels. But Susan Nipper gallantly maintains her point. She keeps a smiling face upon her mistress, smiling through her tears, until the last. Even when she is left behind, the Captain continues to appear and disappear at the door, crying 'Hooroar, my lad! Hooroar, my Heart's Delight!' with his shirt collar in a violent state of agitation, until it is hopeless to attempt to keep up with the coach any longer. Finally, when the coach is gone, Susan Nipper, being rejoined by the Captain, falls into a state of insensibility, and is taken into a baker's shop to recover.

CHARLES DICKENS (1812–1870)
Dombey & Son, Chap. 57

F

THE BASHFULL BRIDE

Now, now's the time; so oft by truth
Promis'd sho'd come to crown your youth.
   Then Faire ones, doe not wrong
   Your joyes, by staying long:
   Or let Love's fire goe out,
   By ling'ring thus in doubt:
   But learn, that Time once lost,
   Is ne'r redeem'd by cost.
Then away; come, Hymen guide
To the bed, the bashfull Bride.

Is it (sweet maid) your fault, these holy
Bridall-Rites goe on so slowly?
   Deare, is it this you dread,
   The losse of Maiden-head?
   Beleeve me; you will most
   Esteeme it when 'tis lost:
   Then it no longer keep,
   Lest Issue lye asleep.
Then away; come, Hymen guide
To the bed, the bashfull Bride.

These Precious-Pearly-Purling tears,
But spring from ceremonious feares.
   And 'tis but Native shame,
   That hides the loving flame:
   And may a while controule
   The soft and am'rous soule;
   But yet, Love's fire will wast
   Such bashfulnesse at last.
Then away; come, Hymen guide
To the bed, the bashfull Bride.

Behold! how Hymen's Taper-light
Shews you how much is spent of night.
    See, see the Bride-groom's Torch
    Halfe wasted in the porch,
    And now those Tapers five,
    That shew the womb shall thrive:
    Their silv'rie flames advance,
    To tell all prosp'rous chance
Still shall crown the happy life
Of the good man and the wife.

ROBERT HERRICK (1591–1674)
From an Epithalamie to Sir Thomas
Southwell and His Lady. *Hesperides*.

SIMILAR ADVICE

Gather ye Rose-buds while ye may,
    Old Time is still a-flying:
And this same flower that smiles to day,
    To morrow will be dying.

The glorious Lamp of Heaven, the Sun,
    The higher he's a-getting;
The sooner will his Race be run,
    And nearer he's to Setting.

That Age is best, which is the first,
When Youth and Blood are warmer;
But being spent, the worse, and worst
    Times, still succeed the former.

Then be not coy, but use your time;
    And while ye may, goe marry:
For having lost but once your prime,
    You may for ever tarry.

ROBERT HERRICK (1591–1674)
To the Virgins. To make much of
Time. *Hesperides.*

It may be worth adding that Herrick included in one of his salutes to a wedding two of the strangest lines to be found in our literature of matrimony:

And thousand gladly wish
You multiply, as doth a Fish.

Apart from the fact that it takes two fishes to multiply, one wonders whether the poet had any idea of the extent of piscine productivity in spawning and of the infant mortality which ensues. Did Herrick ever eat herrings? The sinister hope, attributed to thousands, occurs in 'A Nuptiall Song or Epithalamie on Sir Clipseby Crew and his Lady'.

MATRIMONIAL EPIDEMIC

Enter Dr. Daly, Vicar of Ploverleigh.

Dr. Daly (musing). It is singular—it is very singular. It has overthrown all my calculations. It is distinctly opposed to the doctrine of averages. I cannot understand it.

Aline. Dear Dr. Daly, what has puzzled you?

Dr. Daly. My dear, this village has not hitherto been addicted to marrying and giving in marriage. Hitherto the youths of this village have not been enterprising, and the maidens have been distinctly coy. Judge then of my surprise when I tell you that the whole village came to me in a body just now, and implored me to join them in matrimony with as little delay as possible. Even your excellent father has hinted to me that before very long it is not unlikely that he, also, may change his condition.

Aline. Oh Alexis—do you hear that? Are you not delighted?

Alexis. Yes. I confess that a union between your mother and my father would be a happy circumstance indeed. (*Crossing to Dr. Daly.*) My dear sir—the news that you bring us is very gratifying.

Dr. Daly. Yes—still, in my eyes, it has its melancholy side. This universal marrying recalls the happy days—now, alas, gone for ever—when I myself might have—but tush! I am puling. I am too old to marry—and yet, within the last half hour, I have greatly yearned for companionship. I never remarked it before, but the young maidens of this village are very comely. So likewise are the middle-aged. Also the elderly. All are comely—and (*with a deep sigh*) all are engaged!

Aline. Here comes your father.

Enter Sir Marmaduke with Mrs. Partlet, the pew-opener,
arm-in-arm.

Aline and Alexis (aside). Mrs. Partlet!

Sir Marmaduke. Dr. Daly, give me joy. Alexis, my dear boy, you will, I am sure, be pleased to hear that my declining days are not unlikely to be solaced by the companionship of this good, virtuous, and amiable woman.

Alexis (rather taken aback). My dear father, this is not altogether what I expected. I am certainly taken somewhat by surprise. Still it can hardly be necessary to assure you that any wife of yours is a mother of mine. (*Aside to Aline*) It is not quite what I could have wished.

Mrs. Partlet (crossing to Alexis). Oh sir, I entreat your forgiveness. I am aware that socially I am not heverythink that could be desired, nor am I blessed with an abundance of worldly goods, but I can at least confer on your estimable father the great and priceless dowry of a true, tender, and lovin' 'art!

Alexis (coldly). I do not question it. After all, a faithful love is the true source of every earthly joy.

Sir Marmaduke. I knew that my boy would not blame his poor father for acting on the impulse of a heart that has never yet misled him. Zorah is not pehaps what the world calls beautiful—

Dr. Daly. Still she is comely—distinctly comely! (*Sighs.*)

Aline. Zorah is very good, and very clean, and honest: and quite, quite sober in her habits, and that is worth far more than beauty, dear Sir Marmaduke.

Dr. Daly. Yes; beauty will fade and perish, but personal cleanliness is practically undying, for it can be renewed whenever it discovers symptoms of decay. My dear Sir Marmaduke, I heartily congratulate you. (*Sighs.*)

Quintette
(*Alexis, Aline, Sir Marmaduke, Zorah, and Dr. Daly*)

Alexis
I rejoice that it's decided,
　　Happy now will be his life,
For my father is provided
　　With a true and tender wife.

Ensemble

She will tend him, nurse him, mend him,
　　Air his linen, dry his tears;
Bless the thoughtful fates that send him
　　Such a wife to soothe his years:

Aline

No young giddy thoughtless maiden,
　　Full of graces, airs, and jeers—
But a sober widow, laden
　　With the weight of fifty years!

Sir Marmaduke

No highborn exacting beauty,
　　Blazing like a jewelled sun—
But a wife who'll do her duty,
　　As that duty should be done!

Mrs. Partlet

I'm no saucy minx and giddy—
　　Hussies such as them abound—
But a clean and tidy widdy
　　Well be-known for miles around!

Dr. Daly

All the village now have mated,
　　All are happy as can be—
I to live alone am fated:
　　No one's left to marry me!

SIR W. S. GILBERT (1836–1911)
The Sorcerer, Act 2

WORDSWORTH GIVES WARNING

What need of clamorous bells, or ribands gay,
These humble nuptials to proclaim or grace?
Angels of love, look down upon the place;
Shed on the chosen vale a sun-bright day!
Yet no proud gladness would the Bride display
Even for such promise:—serious is her face,
Modest her mien; and she, whose thoughts keep pace
With gentleness, in that becoming way
Will thank you. Faultless does the Maid appear;
No disproportion in her soul, no strife:
But, when the closer view of wedded life
Hath shown that nothing human can be clear
From frailty, for that insight may the Wife
To her indulgent Lord become more dear.

WILLIAM WORDSWORTH (1770–1850)

This sonnet, with its cautionary close, was written for the marriage at Grasmere of the poet's brother-in-law, Thomas Hutchinson to Mary Monkhouse in 1812.

SOLD IN MARRIAGE

For Ouida the human moths are lured by the bright lights of vicious extravagance. In her novel *Moths*, Lady Dolly had married a nobly born but sincere clergyman called Herbert. On his death she quickly wedded the wealthy Mr. Vanderdecken. But even his riches did not suffice for her prodigal spending. So she contrived to betroth her astoundingly beautiful but virtuous daughter, Vera Herbert, to a debauched but immensely wealthy Russian, Prince Zouroff. Vera, still only sixteen, had lost her heart to 'her nightingale', the greatest tenor singer of the day, who was also of noble birth. But the sale of Vera, with a gigantic marriage settlement, went on so that Lady Dolly could live on champagne and take the stimulant then fashionable, ether. Vera was finally united with her nightingale after the Prince had shot the songster through the throat in a duel, thus silencing his career but leaving him heart-whole. Ouida described the Sins of Society and lashed them with equal gusto. In her absurdity she was always readable.

'Do you believe in wicked people, miladi?' Zouroff said the next evening to Lady Dolly, as they sat together in a box at the Bouffes.

'Wicked people? Oh dear, no—at least—yes,' said Lady Dolly vaguely. 'Yes, I suppose I do. I am afraid one must. One sees dreadful things in the papers; in society everybody is very much like everybody else—no?'

Zouroff laughed; the little, short, hard laugh that was characteristic of him.

'I think one need not go to the papers. I think you and I are both doing evil enough to satisfy the devil—if a devil there be. But, if you do not mind it, I need not.'

Lady Dolly was startled, then smiled.

'What droll things you say! And do not talk so of the——. It doesn't sound well. It's an old-fashioned belief, I know, and not probable, they say, now, but still—one never can tell—'

And Lady Dolly, quite satisfied with herself, laughed her last laugh at the fun of the *Belle Helène*, and had her cloak folded round her, and went out on the arm of her future son-in-law.

Such few great ladies as were already in Paris, passing through from the channel coast to the Riviera, or from one chateau to another, all envied her, she knew; and if anybody had ever said anything that was—that was not quite nice— nobody could say anything now when in another fortnight her daughter would be Princess Zouroff.

'Really, I never fancied at all I was clever, but I begin to think that I am,' she said in her self-complacency to herself.

The idea that she could be wicked seemed quite preposterous to her when she thought it over. 'Harmless little me', she said to herself. True, she had felt wicked when she had met her daughter's eye, but that was nonsense; the qualm had always gone away when she had taken her champagne at dinner or her ether in her bedroom.

A fortnight later the marriage of the head of the house of Zouroff was solemnised at the chapel of the English Embassy and the Russian church in Paris.

Nothing was forgotten that could add to the splendour and pomp of the long ceremonies and sacraments; all that was greatest in the great world was assembled in honour of the event. The gifts were magnificent, and the extravagance un- bridled. The story of the *corbeille* read like a milliner's dream of heaven; the jewels given by the bridegroom were estimated at a money value of millions of roubles, and with them were given the title-deeds of a French estate called Felicité, a free gift of love above and outside all the superb donations con- tained in the settlements. All these things and many more were set forth at length in all the journals of society, and the marriage was one of the great events of the closing year. The only details that the papers did not chronicle were that when the mother, with her tender eyes moist with tears, kissed her daughter, the daughter put her aside without an answering caress, and that when the last words of the sacrament were spoken, she, who had now become the Princess Zouroff, fell forward on the altar in a dead swoon, from which for some time she could not be awakened.

*

Between the Gulf of Villafranca and that of Eza there was a white, shining, sunlit house, with gardens that were in the dreariest month of the year rich and red with roses, golden with orange fruit, and made stately by palms of long growth, through whose stems the blue sea shone. To these gardens there was a long terrace of white marble stretching along the edge of the cliff, with the waves beating far down below; to the terrace there were marble seats and marble steps, and copies of the Loves and Fauns of the Vatican and of the Capitol, with the glow of geraniums flamelike about their feet.

Up and down the length of this stately place a woman moved with a step that was slow and weary, and yet very restless; the step of a thing that is chained. The woman was very young, and very pale; her skirts of olive velvet swept the white stone; her fair hair was coiled loosely with a golden arrow run through it; round her throat there were strings of pearls, the jewels of morning. All women envied her the riches of which those pearls were emblem. She was Vera, Princess Zouroff.

Vera always, now.

She moved up and down, up and down, fatiguing herself, and unconscious of fatigue; the sunny world was quiet about her; the greyhound paced beside her, keeping step with hers. She was alone, and there was no one to look upon her face and see its pain, its weariness, its disgust.

Only a week ago, she thought; only a week since she had fallen in a swoon at the altar of the Russian church; only a week since she had been the girl Vera Herbert. Only a week!— and it seemed to her that thousands of years had come and gone, parting her by ages from that old sweet season of ignorance, of innocence, of peace, of youth.

She was only sixteen still, but she was no more young. Her girlhood had been killed in her as a spring blossom is crushed by a rough hot hand that, meaning to caress it, kills it.

A great disgust filled her, and seemed to suffocate her with its loathing and its shame. Everything else in her seemed dead, except that one bitter sense of intolerable revulsion. All the revolted pride in her was like a living thing buried under a weight of sand, and speechless, but aghast and burning.

'How could she? how could she?' she thought every hour of the day; and the crime of her mother against her seemed the vilest the earth could hold.

She herself had not known what she had done when she had consented to give herself in marriage, but her mother had known.

Poets in all time have poured out their pity on the woman who wakes to a loveless dishonour; what can the few words of a priest, or the envy of a world, do to lighten that shame to sacrificed innocence?—nothing.

Her life had changed as suddenly as a flower changes when the hot sirocco blows over it, and fills it with sand instead of dew. Nothing could help her. Nothing could undo what had been done. Nothing could make her ever more the clear-eyed, fair-souled child that had not even known the meaning of any shame.

'God himself could not help me!' she thought with a bitterness of resignation that was more hopeless than that of the martyrs of old; and she paced up and down the marble road of the terrace, wondering how long her life would last like this.

All the magnificence that surrounded her was hateful; all the gifts that were heaped on her were like insult; all the congratulations that were poured out on her were like the mockeries of apes, like the crackling of dead leaves. In her own sight, and without sin of her own, she had become vile.

And it was only a week ago!

Society would have laughed.

Society had set its seal of approval upon this union, and upon all such unions, and so deemed them sanctified. Year after year, one on another, the pretty, rosy, golden-curled daughters of fair mothers were carefully tended and cultured and reared up to grace the proud races from which they sprang, and were brought out into the great world in their first bloom like half-opened roses, with no other end or aim set before them as the one ambition of their lives than to make such a marriage as this. Whosoever achieved such was blessed.

Pollution? Prostitution? Society would have closed its ears to such words, knowing nothing of such things, not choosing to know anything.

Ouida (Marie Louise de la Ramée)
(1839–1908)
Moths, From Chaps. X and XI

FOOD AND SERVICE

Sumptuous was the feast Nokomis
Made at Hiawatha's wedding.
All the bowls were made of bass-wood,
White and polished very smoothly,
All the spoons of horn of bison,
Black and polished very smoothly,
　She had sent through all the village
Messengers with wands of willow,
As a sign of invitation,
As a token of the feasting;
And the wedding-guests assembled,
Clad in all their richest raiment,
Robes of fur and belts of wampum,
Splendid with their paint and plumage,
Beautiful with beads and tassels.
　First they ate the sturgeon, Nahma,
And the pike, the Maskenozha,
Caught and cooked by old Nokomis;
Then on pemican they feasted,
Pemican and buffalo marrow,
Haunch of deer and hump of bison,
Yellow cakes of the Mondamin,
And the wild rice of the river.
　But the gracious Hiawatha,
And the lovely Laughing Water,
And the careful old Nokomis,
Tasted not the food before them,
Only waited on the others,
Only served their guests in silence.

H. W. LONGFELLOW (1807–1882)
Hiawatha's Wedding Feast

WEDING-DAY SHOPPING

This extract from Thomas Killigrew's *The Parson's Wedding* comes from the end of a Caroline piece which is heavily gross in the main, abounding in a freedom of speech and jesting which lacks the wit and elegance of the better Restoration writers while sharing their favourite subject-matter. Killigrew, who had been page to Charles I, was appointed to the office of Groom of the Bedchamber to Charles II. He built the first Drury Lane Theatre, known as the King's House, under Royal Charter. *The Parson's Wedding* was there revived in 1664, 'acted by nothing but women' and reported by Pepys, not easily shocked, to be loose and obscene. The following passage can cause no alarm: it gives a lively picture of what is now called 'a shopping spree' and of some borrowing before a wedding-feast. The Joseph Taylor mentioned had succeeded Richard Burbage as the leading player of the King's men, Shakespeare's one-time 'fellowship'.

Enter Fiddlers, Jolly, and Wanton.

Jolly. Oh, are you ready, are you ready?

Fiddlers. Yes, an't like your worship.

Jolly. And did you bid the cook chop lustily and make a noise?

Fiddlers. Yes, sir, he's at it.

Wanton. I hear the Captain.

Enter Captain.

Jolly. Have you brought clothes and ribands?

Captain. Yes, yes, all is ready. Did you hear them squeak yet?

Wanton. No, by this light. I think 'tis an appointment and we have been all abused.

Captain. Give the fiddlers their ribands and carry the rest in. Mistress Wanton, you must play my lady's woman today and mince it to all that come, and hold up your head finely when they kiss you, and take heed of swearing when you are angry, and pledging whole cups when they drink to you.

Wanton. I'll warrant you for my part.

Captain. Go get you in then and let your husband dip the rosemary.

Jolly. Is all ready?

Captain. All, all. Some of the company are below already. I have so blown it about. One porter is gone to the Exchange to invite Master Wild's merchant to his wedding, and by the way to bid two or three fruiterers to send in fruit for such a wedding; another in my lady's name to Sall's, for sweet-meats. I swore at Bradborn in his shop myself that I wondered he would disappoint Master Wild for his points, and having so long warning. He protested 'twas not his fault but they were ready and he would send John with them presently. One of the watermen is gone to the melon garden, the other to Cook's at the Bear for some bottles of his best wine, and thence to Gracious Street to the poulterers, and all with directions to send in provisions for Master Wild's wedding. And who should I meet at door but Apricock Tom and Mary, waiting to speak with her young master. They came to beg that they might serve the feast. I promised them they should if they would cry it up and down the town, to bring company, for Master Wild was resolved to keep open house.

Jolly. Why then, here will be witnesses enough.

Captain. But who should I meet at the corner of the Piazza but Joseph Taylor? He tells me there's a new play at the Friars today and I have bespoke a box for Master Wild and his bride.

Jolly. And did he wonder to hear he was married?

Captain. Yes, but I told him 'twas a match his aunt made for him when he was abroad.

Jolly. And I have spread it sufficiently at court by sending to borrow plate for such a wedding.

Enter a Servant.

Servant. There's half a dozen coachfuls of company lighted. They call for the bride-laces and points.

Captain. Let the fiddlers play then, and bid God give them joy, by the name of my Lady Careless and Mistress Wild.

THOMAS KILLIGREW (1612–1683)
The Parson's Wedding, Act V, Scene 1

BELLS AND BUBBLY

But where is she, the bridal flower,
  That must be made a wife ere noon?
  She enters, glowing like the moon
Of Eden on its bridal bower:

On me she bends her blissful eyes
  And then on thee; they meet thy look
  And brighten like the star that shook
Betwixt the palms of paradise.

O when her life was yet in bud,
  He too foretold the perfect rose.
  For thee she grew, for thee she grows
For ever, and as fair as good.

And thou art worthy; full of power;
  As gentle; liberal-minded, great,
  Consistent; wearing all that weight
Of learning lightly like a flower.

But now set out; the noon is near,
  And I must give away the bride;
  She fears not, or with thee beside
And me behind her, will not fear.

Now sign your names, which shall be read,
  Mute symbols of a joyful morn,
  By village eyes as yet unborn;
The names are sign'd, and overhead

Begins the clash and clang that tells
  The joy to every wandering breeze;
  The blind wall rocks, and on the trees
The dead leaf trembles to the bells.

G

O happy hour, and happier hours
    Await them. Many a merry face
    Salutes them—maidens of the place,
That pelt us in the porch with flowers.

O happy hour, behold the bride
    With him to whom her hand I gave.
    They leave the porch, they pass the grave
That has to-day its sunny side.

To-day the grave is bright for me,
    For them the light of life increased,
    Who stay to share the morning feast,
Who rest to-night beside the sea.

Let all my genial spirits advance
    To meet and greet a whiter sun;
    My drooping memory will not shun
The foaming grape of eastern France.

It circles round, and fancy plays,
    And hearts are warm'd and faces bloom,
    As drinking health to bride and groom
We wish them store of happy days.

Nor count me all to blame if I
    Conjecture of a stiller guest,
    Perchance, perchance, among the rest,
And, tho' in silence, wishing joy.

But they must go, the time draws on,
    And those white-favour'd horses wait;
    They rise, but linger; it is late;
Farewell, we kiss, and they are gone.

ALFRED, LORD TENNYSON (1809–1892)
In Memoriam, CXXXI

'IT DON'T TAKE LONG'

When Nicholas Nickleby was recruited as actor and play-wright to the 'Dramatic Corps' of Mr. Vincent Crummles at Portsmouth there came, as an extra attraction, Miss Henrietta Petowker 'of the Theatre Royal, Drury Lane'. Described by Mr. Crummles as 'the only sylph I ever saw who could stand on one leg and play the tambourine on her other knee, like a sylph' Miss Petowker was followed for purposes of marriage by Mr. Lillyvick, a London water-rate collector. The wedding took place at Portsmouth with the Corps in full attendance.

But, perhaps the appearance of Mr. Crummles was more striking and appropriate than that of any member of the party. This gentleman, who personated the bride's father, had, in pursuance of a happy and original conception, "made up" for the part by arraying himself in a theatrical wig, of a style and pattern commonly known as a brown George, and moreover assuming a snuff-coloured suit, of the previous century, with grey silk stockings, and buckles to his shoes. The better to support his assumed character he had determined to be greatly overcome, and, consequently, when they entered the church, the sobs of the affectionate parent were so heartrending that the pew-opener suggested the propriety of his retiring to the vestry, and comforting himself with a glass of water before the ceremony began.

The procession up the aisle was beautiful. The bride, with the four bridesmaids, forming a group previously arranged and rehearsed; the collector, followed by his second, imitating his walk and gestures, to the indescribable amusement of some theatrical friends in the gallery; Mr. Crummles, with an infirm and feeble gait; Mrs. Crummles advancing with that stage walk, which consists of a stride and a stop alternately; it was the completest thing ever witnessed. The ceremony was very quickly disposed of, and all parties present having signed the register (for which purpose, when it came to his turn, Mr. Crummles carefully wiped and put on an immense pair of

spectacles), they went back to breakfast in high spirits. And
here they found Nicholas awaiting their arrival.

'Now then,' said Crummles, who had been assisting Mrs.
Grudden in the preparations, which were on a more extensive
scale than was quite agreeable to the collector, 'Breakfast,
breakfast.'

No second invitation was required. The company crowded
and squeezed themselves at the table as well as they could, and
fell to, immediately; Miss Petowker blushing very much when
anybody was looking, and eating very much when anybody
was *not* looking; and Mr. Lillyvick going to work as though
with the cool resolve, that since the good things must be paid
for by him, he would leave as little as possible for the
Crummleses to eat up afterwards.

'It's very soon done, sir, isn't it?' inquired Mr. Folair of
the collector, leaning over the table to address him.

'What is soon done, sir?' returned Mr. Lillyvick.

'The tying up, the fixing oneself with a wife,' replied Mr.
Folair. 'It don't take long, does it?'

'No, sir,' replied Mr. Lillyvick, colouring. 'It does not take
long. And what then, sir?'

'Oh, nothing,' said the actor. 'It don't take a man long to
hang himself, either, eh? Ha, ha!'

Mr. Lillyvick laid down his knife and fork, and looked
round the table with indignant astonishment.

'To hang himself!' repeated Mr. Lillyvick.

A profound silence came upon all, for Mr. Lillyvick was
dignified beyond expression.

'To hang himself!' cried Mr. Lillyvick again. 'Is any
parallel attempted to be drawn in this company between
matrimony and hanging?'

'The noose, you know,' said Mr. Folair, a little crestfallen.

'The noose, sir?' retorted Mr. Lillyvick. 'Does any man
dare to speak to me of a noose, and Henrietta Pe . . .'

'Lillyvick,' suggested Mr. Crummles.

'. . . and Henrietta Lillyvick in the same breath?' said the
collector. 'In this house, in the presence of Mr. and Mrs.

Crummles, who have brought up a talented and virtuous family, to be blessings and phenomenons, and what not, are we to hear talk of nooses?'

'Folair,' said Mr. Crummles, deeming it a matter of decency to be affected by this allusion to himself and partner, 'I'm astonished at you.'

'What are you going on in this way at me for?' urged the unfortunate actor. 'What have I done?'

'Done, sir!' cried Mr. Lillyvick, 'aimed a blow at the whole framework of society . . .'

'And the best and tenderest feelings,' added Crummles, relapsing into the old man.

'And the highest and most estimable of social ties,' said the collector. 'Noose! As if one was caught, trapped, into the married state, pinned by the leg, instead of going into it of one's own accord and glorying in the act!'

'I didn't mean to make it out, that you were caught and trapped and pinned by the leg,' replied the actor. 'I'm sorry for it; I can't say any more.'

'So you ought to be, sir,' returned Mr. Lillyvick; 'and I am glad to hear that you have enough feeling left to be so.'

The quarrel appearing to terminate with this reply, Mrs. Lillyvick considered that the fittest occasion (the attention of the company being no longer distracted) to burst into tears, and require the assistance of all four bridesmaids, which was immediately rendered, though not without some confusion, for the room being small and the table-cloth long, a whole detachment of plates were swept off the board at the very first move. Regardless of this circumstance, however, Mrs. Lillyvick refused to be comforted until the belligerents had passed their words that the dispute should be carried no further.

CHARLES DICKENS (1812–1870)
Nicholas Nickelby, Chap. 25

RIVERSIDE BRIDES

Calm was the day, and through the trembling air
Sweet-breathing Zephyrus did softly play—
A gentle spirit, that lightly did delay
Hot Titan's beams, which then did glister fair:
When I, (whom sullen care,
Through discontent of my long fruitless stay
In princes' court, and expectation vain
Of idle hopes, which still do fly away
Like empty shadows, did afflict my brain)
Walk'd forth to ease my pain
Along the shore of silver-streaming Thames;
Whose rutty bank, the which his river hems,
Was painted all with variable flowers,
And all the meads adorn'd with dainty gems
Fit to deck maidens' bowers,
And crown their paramours
Against the bridal day, which is not long:
　　Sweet Thames! run softly, till I end my song.

There in a meadow by the river's side
A flock of nymphs I chancéd to espy,
All lovely daughters of the flood thereby,
With goodly greenish locks all loose untied
As each had been a bride;
And each one had a little wicker basket
Made of fine twigs, entrailéd curiously,
In which they gather'd flowers to fill their flasket,
And with fine fingers cropt full feateously
The tender stalks on high.
Of every sort which in that meadow grew
They gather'd some; the violet, pallid blue,
The little daisy that at evening closes,

The virgin lily and the primrose true,
With store of vermeil roses,
To deck their bridegrooms' posies
Against the bridal day, which was not long:
　　Sweet Thames! run softly, till I end my song.

At length they all to merry London came,
To merry London, my most kindly nurse,
That to me gave this life's first native source,
Though from another place I take my name,
An house of ancient fame:
There when they came whereas those bricky towers
The which on Thames' broad aged back do ride,
Where now the studious lawyers have their bowers,
There whilome wont the Templar-knights to bide,
Till they decay'd through pride;
Next whereunto there stands a stately place,
Where oft I gainéd gifts and goodly grace
Of that great lord, which therein wont to dwell,
Whose want too well now feeds my friendless case;
But ah! here fits not well
Old woes, but joys to tell
Against the bridal way, which is not long:
　　Sweet Thames! run softly, till I end my song.

Yet therein now doth lodge a noble peer,
Great England's glory and the world's wide wonder,
Whose dreadful name late through all Spain did thunder,
And Hercules' two pillars standing near
Did make to quake and fear:
Fair branch of honour, flower of chivalry!
That fillest England with thy triumphs' fame
Joy have thou of thy noble victory.
And endless happiness of thine own name
That promiseth the same;
That through thy prowess and victorious arms
Thy country may be freed from foreign harms,

And great Elisa's glorious name may ring
Through all the world, fill'd with thy wide alarms,
Which some brave Muse may sing
To ages following:
Upon the bridal day, which is not long:
  Sweet Thames! run softly, till I end my song.

From those high towers this noble lord issuing
Like radiant Hesper, when his golden hair
In th' ocean billows he hath bathed fair,
Descended to the river's open viewing
With a great train ensuing.
Above the rest were goodly to be seen
Two gentle knights of lovely face and feature,
Beseeming well the bower of any queen,
With gifts of wit and ornaments of nature,
Fit for so goodly stature,
That like the twins of Jove they seem'd in sight
Which deck the baldric of the Heavens bright;
They two, forth pacing to the river's side,
Received those two fair brides, their love's delight;
Which, at th' appointed tide,
Each one did make his bride
Against their bridal day, which is not long:
  Sweet Thames! run softly, till I end my song.

EDMUND SPENSER (1553–1598)
From *Prothalamion*

The noble peer, as radiant as Hesper, was the Earl of Worcester whose two daughters married Henry Gifford and William Peter.

SONG AND DANCE IN THE MEARNS

———•◦✦◈✦◦•———

A Scots Quair tells the story of Chris Guthrie, the daughter of a small farmer in the Mearns, where, just south of Aberdeen, the hills roll down to the sea. Chris marries Ewan Tavendale and the local crofters and characters come to the wedding.

Lewis Grassic Gibbon was a pen-name used by Leslie Mitchell for his later and essentially Scottish writing. He was himself the son of a farmer in the Mearns and wrote of the life he knew as a boy, 'the springs and winters of this land and all the sounds and scents of it', where the Last of the Peasants, as he called them, lived sparely but not too sadly on their small hard-worked, horse-worked pieces of land 'before the coming of the great machines and the great herds'. 'The crofter has gone,' he wrote, 'the man with the house and the steading of his own and the land closer to his heart than the flesh of his body.'

Mitchell went to Stonehaven Academy, became a journalist and novelist. He was just reaching his best as a painter of the Scotland he had known when death overtook him at the age of thirty-four. The wedding party here described is in mid-winter in Blawearie.

No sooner was the dancing done than there were cries 'Rob, what about a song now, man?' And Rob said 'Och, ay, I'll manage that fine,' and he off with his coat and loosened his collar and sang them Ladies of Spain; and then he turned round to where Chris stood beside her Ewan and sang 'The Lass that Made the Bed to Me':

> Her hair was like the link o' gowd,
>   Her teeth were like the ivorie,
> Her cheeks like lilies dipt in wine,
>   The lass that made the bed to me.

> Her bosom was the driven snaw,
>   Two drifted heaps sae fair to see,
> Her limbs, the polished marble stane,
>   The lass that made the bed to me.

I kissed her owre and owre again,
  And aye she wist na what to say,
I laid her between me and the wa',
  The lassie thought na long till day.

Folk stared and nodded at Chris while Rob was singing and
Ewan looked at first as though he'd like to brain him; and
then he blushed; but Chris just listened and didn't care, she
thought the song fine and the lass lovely, she hoped she herself
would seem as lovely this night—or as much of it as their
dancing would leave. So she clapped Rob and syne it was
Ellison's turn, he stood up with his meikle belly a-wag and
sang them a song they didn't know:

Roses and lilies her cheeks disclose,
  But her red lips are sweeter than those,
Kiss her, caress her,
  With blisses her kisses,
Dissolve us in pleasure and soft repose.

and then another, an English one and awful sad, about a young
childe called Villikins and a quean called Dinah, and it
finished:

For a cup of cold pizen lay there on the ground

.   .   .   .

With a tooril-i-ooril-i-oorily-i-ay.

Chae cried that was hardly the kind of thing that they
wanted, woeful as that; and they'd better give Chris a rest
about her roses and lips and limbs, she had them all in safe-
keeping, and would know how to use them; and what about
a seasonable song? And he sang so that all joined in seasonable
enough, for the snow had come on again in spite of the frost:

Up in the morning's no for me,
  Up in the morning early,
When a' the hills are covered wi' snaw
  I'm sure it's winter fairly!

Then Mistress Mutch sang, that was hardly expected, and folk tittered a bit; but she had as good a voice as most and better than some, she sang 'The Bonnie House o' Airlie', and then the 'Auld Robin Grey' that aye brought Chris near to weeping, and did now, and not her alone, with Rob's fiddle whispering it out, the sadness and the soreness of it, though it was long, long syne:

When the sheep are in the fauld, and the kye are a' at hame
And a' the weary world to its rest has gane,
The tears o' my sorrow fa' in shooers frae my e'e
And Auld Robin Gray he lies sound by me.

and all the tale of young Jamie who went to sea and was thought to be drownded in an awful storm; and his lass married Auld Robin Gray and syne Jamie came back but couldn't win his lass away from the auld man, though near brokenhearted she was:

I gang like a ghaist, and I carena' to spin,
I daurna' think o' Jamie, for that wad be a sin,
But I'll try aye my best a guid wife to be,
For Auld Robin Gray he is kind to me.

Old Pooty was sleeping in a corner; he woke up then, fell keen to recite his 'Timrous Beastie'; but they pulled him down and cried on the bride herself for a song. And all she could think of was that south country woman crying in the night by the side of her good man, the world asleep and grey without; and she whispered the song to Rob and he tuned his fiddle and she sang, facing them, young and earnest, and she saw Ewan looking at her solemn and proud, 'The Flowers of the Forest':

I've heard them lilting at our ewe-milking,
Lasses a' lilting before dawn o' day;
But now they are moaning on ilka green loaning,
The Flooers o' the Forest are a' wede away.

Dool and wae for the order sent oor lads tae the Border!
The English for ance, by guile wan the day,
The Flooers o' the Forest, that fought aye the foremost,
The pride o' oor land lie cauld in the clay.

Chae jumped up when she finished, he said "Damn't, folk,
we'll all have the whimsies if we listen to any more woesome
songs! Have none of you a cheerful one?' And the folk in the
barn laughed at him and shook their heads, it came on Chris
how strange was the sadness of Scotland's singing, made for
the sadness of the land and sky in dark autumn evenings, the
crying of men and women of the land who had seen their lives
and loves sink away in the years, things wept for beside the
sheep-buchts, remembered at night and in twilight. The
gladness and kindness had passed, lived and forgotten, it was
Scotland of the mist and rain and the crying sea that made the
songs—And Chae cried 'Let's have another dance, then, it's
nearly a quarter to twelve, we must all be off soon as midnight,
chaps.'

And they all minded what midnight would bring, and Chae
and Rob had the melodeon and fiddle in hand again, and
struck up an eightsome, and everybody grabbed him a partner,
it didn't matter who was who, McIvor had Chris and danced
with her as though he would like to squeeze her to death, he
danced light as thistle-down, the great red Highlander; and
no sooner was one dance finished than Rob and Chae swept
forward into another, they played like mad and the lights
whipped and jumped as the couples spun round and round;
and the music went out across the snowing night; and then
Chae pulled out his great silver watch, and laid it beside him,
playing on.

And suddenly it was the New Year, and the dancing stopped
and folk all shook hands, coming to shake Chris's and Ewan's;
and Long Rob struck up the sugary surge of 'Auld Lang Syne'
and they all joined hands and stood in a circle to sing it, and
Chris thought of Will far over the seas in Argentine, under the
hot night there. Then the singing finished, they all found

themselves tired, somebody began to take down the barn
lights, there was half an hour's scramble of folk getting themselves into coats and getting their shivering sholts from out the
empty stalls in the byre. Then Chris and Ewan were handshook
again, Chris's arm began to ache, and then the last woof-woof
of wheels on snow thick-carpeted came up the Blawearie road
to them, it was fell uncanny that silence in the place after all
the noise and fun of the long, lit hours. And there was Mistress
Melon in the kitchen-door, yawning fit to swallow a horse, she
whispered to Chris 'I'm taking your room now, don't forget,'
and cried them 'Good night, and a sound sleep, both!' and
was up the stairs and left them alone.

Lewis Grassic Gibbon (1901–1935)

'Sunset Song', first volume of *A Scots Quair*, Chapter 3

SUPPER AND COMPANY

So passd they naked on, nor shund the sight
Of God or Angel, for they thought no ill:
So hand in hand they passd, the lovliest pair
That ever since in loves imbraces met,
Adam the goodliest man of men since born
His Sons, the fairest of her Daughters Eve.
Under a tuft of shade that on a green
Stood whispering soft, by a fresh Fountain side
They sat them down, and after no more toil
Of thir sweet Gardning labour then suffic'd
To recommend coole Zephyr, and made ease
More easie, wholsom thirst and appetite
More grateful, to thir Supper Fruits they fell,
Nectarine Fruits which the compliant boughes
Yeilded them, side-long as they sat recline
On the soft downie Bank damaskt with flours:
The savourie pulp they chew, and in the rinde
Still as they thirsted scoop the brimming stream;
Nor gentle purpose, nor endearing smiles
Wanted, nor youthful dalliance as beseems
Fair couple, linkt in happie nuptial League,
Alone as they. About them frisking playd
All Beasts of th' Earth, since wilde, and of all chase
In Wood or Wilderness, Forrest or Den;
Sporting the Lion ramp'd, and in his paw
Dandl'd the Kid; Bears, Tygers, Ounces, Pards
Gambold before them, th' unwieldy Elephant
To make them mirth us'd all his might, and wreathd
His Lithe Proboscis; close the Serpent sly
Insinuating, wove with Gordian twine
His breaded train, and of his fatal guile

Gave proof unheeded; others in the grass
Coucht, and now fild with pasture gazing sat,
Or Bedward ruminating.

JOHN MILTON (1608–1674)
Paradise Lost, Book IV

THE POET REJECTED

The scene is Castle Bunthorne. Enter to Reginald Bunthorne, a Fleshly Poet, Patience the innocent milk-maid.

Bunthorne. Ah! Patience, come hither. I am pleased with thee, The bitter-hearted one, who finds all else hollow, is pleased with thee. For you are not hollow. *Are* you?

Patience. I beg your pardon—I interrupt you.

Bunthorne. Life is made up of interruptions. The tortured soul, yearning for solitude, writhes under them. Oh, but my heart is a-weary! Oh, I am a cursed thing! Don't go.

Patience. Really, I'm very sorry—

Bunthorne. Tell me, girl, do you ever yearn?

Patience (misunderstanding him). I earn my living.

Bunthorne (impatiently). No, no! Do you know what it is to be heart-hungry? Do you know what it is to yearn for the Indefinable, and yet to be brought face to face, daily, with the Multiplication Table? Do you know what it is to seek oceans and to find puddles?—to long for whirlwinds and to have to do the best you can with the bellows? That's my case. Oh, I am a cursed thing!

Patience. If you please, I don't understand you—you frighten me!

Bunthorne. Don't be frightened—it's only poetry.

Patience. If that's poetry, I don't like poetry.

Bunthorne (eagerly), Don't you? *(Aside)* Can I trust her? *(Aloud)* Patience, you don't like poetry—well, between you and me, *I* don't like poetry. It's hollow, unsubstantial—unsatisfactory. What's the use of yearning for Elysian Fields when you know you can't get 'em, and would only let 'em out on building leases if you had 'em?

Patience. Sir, I—

Bunthorne. Don't go. Patience, I have long loved you. Let

me tell you a secret. I am not as bilious as I look. If you like, I will cut my hair. There is more innocent fun within me than a casual spectator would imagine. You have never seen me frolicsome. Be a good girl—a very good girl—and you shall.

Patience. Sir, I will speak plainly. In the matter of love I am untaught. I have never loved but my great-aunt. But I am quite certain that, under any circumstances, I couldn't possibly love *you*.

Bunthorne. Oh, you think not?

Patience. I'm quite sure of it. Quite sure. Quite.

Bunthorne (releasing her). Very good. Life is henceforth a blank. I don't care what becomes of me. I have only to ask that you will not abuse my confidence: though *you* despise me, I am extremely popular with the other young ladies.

Patience. I only ask that you will leave me and never renew the subject.

Bunthorne. Certainly. Broken-hearted and desolate, I go. (*Recites.*)

> "Oh, to be wafted away,
>   From this black Aceldama of sorrow,
>   Where the dust of an earthy to-day
>   Is the earth of a dusty to-morrow!"

It is a little thing of my own. I call it 'Heart Foam'. I shall not publish it. Farewell!   (*Exit Bunthorne.*)

Patience. What on earth does it all mean? Why does he love me? Why does he expect me to love him? He's not a relation! It frightens me!

Sir W. S. GILBERT (1836–1911)
Patience, Act I

H

MONEY IN THE AIR

There is excitement in the Veneering mansion. The mature young lady is going to married (powder and all) to the mature young gentleman, and she is to be married from the Veneering house, and the Veneerings are to give the breakfast. The Analytical, who objects as a matter of principle to everything that occurs on the premises, necessarily objects to the match; but his consent has been dispensed with, and a spring van is delivering its load of greenhouse plants at the door, in order that to-morrow's feast may be crowned with flowers.

The mature young lady is a lady of property. The mature young gentleman is a gentleman of property. He invests his property. He goes, in a condescending amateurish way, into the City, attends meetings of Directors, and has to do with traffic in Shares. As is well known to the wise in their generation, traffic in Shares is the one thing to have to do with in this world. Have no antecedents, no established character, no cultivation, no ideas, no manners; have Shares. Have Shares enough to be on Boards of Direction in capital letters, oscillate on mysterious business between London and Paris, and be great. Where does he come from? Shares. Where is he going to? Shares. What are his tastes? Shares. Has he any principles. Shares. What squeezes him into Parliament? Shares. Perhaps he never of himself achieved success in anything, never originated anything, never produced anything! Sufficient answer to all; Shares. O mighty Shares! To set those blaring images so high, and to cause us smaller vermin, as under the influence of henbane or opium, to cry out night and day, 'Relieve us of our money, scatter it for us, buy us and sell us, ruin us, only we beseech ye take rank among the powers of the earth, and fatten on us!'

*

And now Veneering shoots out of the Study wherein he is

accustomed, when contemplative, to give his mind to the carving and gilding of the Pilgrims going to Canterbury, in order to show Twemlow the little flourish he has prepared for the trumpets of fashion, describing how that on the seventeenth instant, at St. James's Church, the Reverend Blank Blank, assisted by the Reverend Dash Dash, united in the bonds of matrimony, Alfred Lammle, Esquire, of Sackville Street, Piccadilly, to Sophronia, only daughter of the late Horatio Akershem, Esquire, of Yorkshire. Also how the fair bride was married from the house of Hamilton Veneering, Esquire, of Stucconia, and was given away by Melvin Twemlow, Esquire, of Duke Street, St. James's, second cousin to Lord Snigsworth, of Snigsworthy Park. While perusing which composition, Twemlow makes some opaque approach to perceiving that if the Reverend Blank Blank and the Reverend Dash Dash fail, after this introduction, to become enrolled in the list of Veneering's dearest and oldest friends, they will have none but themselves to thank for it.

*

Betimes next morning, that horrible old Lady Tippins (relict of the late Sir Thomas Tippins, knighted in mistake for somebody else by His Majesty King George the Third, who, while performing the ceremony, was graciously pleased to observe, 'What, what, what? Who, who, who? Why, why, why?') begins to be dyed and varnished for the interesting occasion. She has a reputation for giving smart accounts of things, and she must be at these people's early, my dear, to lose nothing of the fun. Whereabout in the bonnet and drapery announced by her name, any fragment of the real woman may be concealed, is perhaps known to her maid; but you could easily buy all you see of her, in Bond Street: or you might scalp her, and peel her, and scrape her, and make two Lady Tippinses out of her, and yet not penetrate to the genuine article. She has a large gold eye-glass, has Lady Tippins, to survey proceedings with. If she had one in each eye, it might keep that other drooping lid up, and look more uniform. But perennial youth is in her artificial flowers, and her list of lovers is full.

'Mortimer, you wretch,' says Lady Tippins, turning the eye-glass about and about, 'where is your charge, the bridegroom?'

'Give you my honour,' returns Mortimer, 'I don't know, and I don't care.'

'Miserable! Is that the way you do your duty?'

'Beyond an impression that he is to sit upon my knees and be seconded at some point of the solemnities, like a principal at a prize-fight, I assure you I have no notion what my duty is,' returns Mortimer.

Eugene is also in attendance, with a pervading air upon him of having presupposed the ceremony to be a funeral, and of being disappointed. The scene is the Vestry-room of St. James's Church, with a number of leathery old registers on shelves, that might be bound in Lady Tippinses.

But, hark! A carriage at the gate, and Mortimer's man arrives, looking rather like a spurious Mephistopheles and an unacknowledged member of that gentleman's family. Whom Lady Tippins, surveying through her eye-glass, considers a fine man, and quite a catch; and of whom Mortimer remarks, in the lowest spirits, as he approaches, 'I believe this is my fellow, confound him!' More carriages at the gate, and lo, the rest of the characters. Whom Lady Tippins, standing on a cushion, surveying through the eye-glass, thus checks off: 'Bride; five-and-forty if a day, thirty shillings a yard, veil fifteen pounds, pocket-handkerchief a present. Bridesmaids; kept down for fear of outshining bride, consequently not girls, twelve and sixpence a yard, Veneering's flowers, snub-nosed one rather pretty but too conscious of her stockings, bonnets, three pound ten. Twemlow; blessed release for the dear man if she really was his daughter, nervous even under the pretence that she is, well he may be. Mrs. Veneering; never saw such velvet, say two thousand pounds as she stands, absolute jeweller's window, father must have been a pawnbroker, or how could these people do it? Attendant unknowns; pokey.'

Ceremony performed, register signed, Lady Tippins

escorted out of sacred edifice by Veneering, carriages rolling back to Stucconia, servants with favours and flowers, Veneering's house reached, drawing-rooms most magnificent. Here, the Podsnaps await the happy party; Mr. Podsnap, with his hair-brushes made the most of; that imperial rocking-horse, Mrs. Podsnap, majestically skittish. Here, too, are Boots and Brewer, and the two other Buffers; each Buffer with a flower in his button-hole, his hair curled, and his gloves buttoned on tight, apparently come prepared, if anything had happened to the bridegroom, to be married instantly. Here, too, the bride's aunt, and next relation; a widowed female of a Medusa sort, in a stony cap, glaring petrifaction at her fellow-creatures. Here, too, the bride's trustee; an oilcake-fed style of business-gentleman with mooney spectacles, and an object of much interest. Veneering launching himself upon this trustee as his oldest friend (which makes seven, Twenlow thought), and confidentially retiring with him into the conservatory, it is understood that Veneering is his co-trustee, and that they are arranging about the Thou-sand Pou-nds! with a smack and a relish suggestive of the very finest oysters. Pokey unknowns, amazed to find how intimately they know Veneering, pluck up spirit, fold their arms, and begin to contradict him before breakfast. What time Mrs. Veneering, carrying baby dressed as a bridesmaid, flits about among the company, emitting flashes of many-coloured lightning from diamonds, emeralds, and rubies.

*

In which state of affairs, the usual ceremonies rather droop and flag, and the splendid cake when cut by the fair hand of the bride has put on an indigestible appearance. However, all the things indispensable to be said are said, and all the things indispensable to be done are done (including Lady Tippins's yawning, falling asleep, and waking insensible), and there is hurried preparation for the nuptial journey to the Isle of Wight, and the outer air teems with brass bands and spectators.

*

And so Lady Tippins, quite undetermined whether to-day is the day before yesterday, or the day after to-morrow, or the week after next, fades away; and Mortimer Lightwood and Eugene fade away, and Twenlow fades away, and the stony aunt goes away—she declines to fade, proving rock to the last—and even the unknowns are slowly strained off, and it is all over.

CHARLES DICKENS (1812–1870)
Our Mutual Friend, Chap. X

BRIDAL SONG

Roses, their sharp spines being gone,
Not royal in their smells alone,
　　But in their hue;
Maiden pinks, of odour faint,
Daisies smell-less, yet most quaint,
　　And sweet thyme true;

Primrose, firstborn child of Ver,
Merry springtime's harbinger,
　　With harebells dim;
Oxlips in their cradles growing
Marigolds on deathbeds blowing,
　　Larks'-heels trim.

All dear Nature's children sweet,
Lie 'fore bride and bridegroom's feet.
　　Blessing their sense!
Not an angel of the air,
Bird melodious, or bird fair,
　　Be absent hence!

The crow, the slanderous cuckoo, nor
The boding raven, nor chough hoar,
　　Nor chattering pie,
May on our bridehouse perch or sing,
Or with them any discord bring,
　　But from it fly!

JOHN FLETCHER (1576–1625)
Song in *The Two Noble Kinsmen*

This play, probably written in 1613, was published in Quarto form in 1634
and described as 'Presented at the Blackfriers by the Kings Maiesties servants,
with great applause: Written by the memorable Worthies of their time; Mr.

John Fletcher, and Mr. William Shakespeare. Gent. Printed at London by Tho. Cotes, for Iohn Waterson: and are to be sold at the signe of the Crowne in Pauls Churchyard. 1634.'

There are strong signs of Shakespeare's hand in several sections of the play and this lyric may be his. The list of flowers includes his favourites. He had recently linked the hare-bell and the primrose in the exquisite lament over Fidele's body in *Cymbeline*.

COMMODORE TRUNNION WEDS

Another day was fixed for the nuptials; and in order to balk the curiosity of idle people, which had given great offence, the parson was prevailed upon to perform the ceremony in the garrison, which all that day was adorned with flags and pendants displayed; and at night illuminated, by the direction of Hatchway, who also ordered the patereroes to be fired, as soon as the marriage-knot was tied. Neither were the other parts of the entertainment neglected by this ingenious contriver, who produced undeniable proofs of his elegance and art in the wedding-supper, which had been committed to his management and direction. This genial banquet was entirely composed of sea-dishes; a huge pillaw, consisting of a large piece of beef sliced, a couple of fowls, and half a peck of rice, smoked in the middle of the board: a dish of hard fish, swimming in oil, appeared at each end; the sides being furnished with a mess of that savoury composition known by the name of lob's-course, and a plate of salmagundy. The second course displayed a goose of a monstrous magnitude, flanked with two Guinea-hens, a pig barbacued, a hock of salt pork in the midst of a pease-pudding, a leg of mutton roasted, with potatoes, and another boiled with yams. The third service was made up of a loin of fresh pork, with apple-sauce, a kid smothered with onions, and a terrapin baked in the shell; and, last of all, a prodigious sea-pie was presented, with an infinite volume of pancakes and fritters. That everything might be answerable to the magnificence of this delicate feast, he had provided vast quantities of strong beer, flip, rumbo, and burnt brandy, with plenty of Barbadoes water for the ladies; and hired all the fiddles within six miles, which, with the addition of a drum, bagpipe, and Welsh harp, regaled the guests with a most melodious concert.

The company, who were not at all exceptious, seemed

extremely well pleased with every particular of the entertainment; and the evening being spent in the most social manner, the bride was by her sister conducted to her apartment, where, however, a trifling circumstance had like to have destroyed the harmony which had been hitherto maintained.

I have already observed, that there was not one standing bed within the walls; therefore the reader will not wonder that Mrs. Trunnion was out of humour when she found herself under the necessity of being confined with her spouse in a hammock, which, though enlarged with a double portion of canvass, and dilated with a yoke for the occasion, was at best but a disagreeable, not to say dangerous, situation. She accordingly complained with some warmth of this inconvenience, which she imputed to disrespect; and, at first, absolutely refused to put up with the expedient: but Mrs. Pickle soon brought her to reason and compliance, by observing that one night would soon be elapsed, and next day she might regulate her own economy.

Thus persuaded, she ventured into the vehicle, and was visited by her husband in less than an hour, the company being departed to their own homes, and the garrison left to the command of his lieutenant and mate. But it seems the hooks that supported this swinging couch were not calculated for the addition of weight which they were now destined to bear; and therefore gave way in the middle of the night, to the no small terror of Mrs. Trunnion, who perceiving herself falling, screamed aloud, and by that exclamation brought Hatchway, with a light into the chamber. Though she had received no injury by the fall, she was extremely discomposed and incensed at the accident, which she even openly ascribed to the obstinacy and whimsical oddity of the commodore, in such petulant terms as evidently declared that she thought her great aim accomplished, and her authority secured against all the shocks of fortune. Indeed her bedfellow seemed to be of the same opinion, by his tacit resignation; for he made no reply to her insinuations, but with a most vinegar aspect crawled out of his nest, and betook himself to rest in another apartment: while his irritated spouse dismissed the lieutenant, and from the wreck of the hammock made an occasional bed for herself on the floor, fully determined to provide better accommodation for the next night's lodging.

TOBIAS SMOLLETT (1721–1771)
Peregrine Pickle, Chap. IX

SERVICE AND TRANSPORT

This was the wedding morn of Priscilla the Puritan maiden.
Friends were assembled together; the Elder and Magistrate also
Graced the scene with their presence, and stood like the Law and the Gospel,
One with the sanction of earth, and one with the blessing of heaven.
Simple and brief was the wedding, as that of Ruth and of Boaz.
Softly the youth and the maiden repeated the words of betrothal,
After the Puritan way, and the laudable custom of Holland.
Fervently then, and devoutly, the excellent Elder of Plymouth
Prayed for the hearth, and the home, that were founded that day in affection,
Speaking of life and of death, and imploring divine benedictions.
  Meanwhile the bridegroom went forth and stood with the bride at the doorway,
Breathing the perfumed air of that warm and beautiful morning.
Touched with autumnal tints, but lonely and sad in the sunshine,
Lay extended before them the land of toil and privation;
There were the graves of the dead, and the barren waste of the sea-shore,
There the familiar fields, the groves of pine, and the meadows;
But to their eyes transfigured, it seemed as the Garden of Eden,
Filled with the presence of God, whose voice was the sound of the ocean.

*

Soon was their vision disturbed by the noise and stir of
    departure,
Friends coming forth from the house, and impatient of longer
    delaying,
Each with his plan for the day, and the work that was left
    uncompleted.
Then from a stall near at hand, amid exclamations of wonder,
Alden the thoughtful, the careful, so happy, so proud of
    Priscilla,
Brought out his snow-white bull, obeying the hand of its
    master,
Led by a cord that was tied to an iron ring in its nostrils,
Covered with crimson cloth, and a cushion placed for a saddle.
She should not walk, he said, through the dust and heat of the
    noon-day;
Nay, she should ride like a queen, not plod along like a
    peasant.
Somewhat alarmed at first, but reassured by the others,
Placing her hand on the cushion, her foot in the hand of her
    husband,
Gaily, with joyous laugh, Priscilla mounted her palfrey.

H. W. LONGFELLOW (1807–1882)
The Courtship of Miles Standish, IX

AT THE REGISTRAR'S

H. G. Wells's Mr. Lewisham, a science student in the eighteen-nineties, married his Ethel with more hope than money for their quiet wedding and meagre honeymoon in London lodgings. They had their dream. They were fellow-combatants against the harsh, unfeeling universe.

The marriage was to take place at two. . . . Suppose she never came at all! After three trains in succession had disappointed him his vague feelings of dread gave place to a profound depression. . . .

But she came at last, and it was twenty-three minutes to two. He hurried her luggage downstairs, booked it with his own, and in another minute they were in a handsom—their first experience of that species of conveyance—on the way to the Registrar's office. They had said scarcely anything to one another, save hasty directions from Lewisham, but their eyes were full of excitement, and under the apron of the cab their hands were gripped together.

The little old gentleman was business-like but kindly. They made their vows to him, to a lean black-bearded clerk and a lady who took off an apron in the nether part of the building to attend. The little old gentleman made no long speeches. 'You are young people,' he said slowly, 'and life together is a difficult thing. . . . Be kind to each other.' He smiled, and held out a friendly hand.

Ethel's eyes glistened and she found she could not speak.

AFTERWARDS

Save for its brevity and these intimations of future trouble it was a very fine time indeed. Their midday dinner together, for example—it was a little cold when at last they came to it on Saturday—was immense fun. There was no marked subsidence of appetite; they ate extremely well in spite of the meeting of their souls, and in spite of certain shiftings of chairs and hand claspings and similar delays. He really made the acquaintance of her hand then for the first time, plump white hands with short white fingers, and the engagement ring had come out of its tender hiding-place and acted as keeper to the wedding ring. Their eyes were perpetually flitting about the room and coming back to mutual smiles. All their movements were faintly tremulous.

She professed to be vastly interested and amused by the room and its furniture and her position, and he was delighted by her delight. She was particularly entertained by the chest of drawers in the living room, and by Lewisham's witticisms at the toilet tidies and the oleographs.

And after the chops and most of the tinned salmon and the very new loaf were gone they fell to with fine effect upon a tapioca pudding. Their talk was fragmentary. 'Did you hear her call me *Madame*? *Mádáme*—so!' And presently I must go out and do some shopping. There are all the things for Sunday and Monday morning to get. I must make a list. It will never do to let her know how little I know about things. . . . I wish I knew more.'

At the time Lewisham regarded her confession of domestic ignorance as a fine basis for facetiousness. He developed a fresh line of thought, and condoled with her on the inglorious circumstances of their wedding. 'No bridesmaids,' he said; 'no little children scattering flowers, no carriages, no policemen to guard the wedding presents, nothing proper—nothing right. Not even a white favour. Only you and I.'

'Only you and I. *Oh!*'

'This is nonsense,' said Lewisham, after an interval.

'And think what we lose in the way of speeches,' he resumed. 'Cannot you imagine the best man rising—'Ladies and gentleman—the health of the bride.' That is what the best man has to do isn't it?'

By way of answer she extended her hand.

'And do you know,' he said, after that had received due recognition, 'we have never been introduced!'

'Neither have we!' said Ethel. 'Neither have we! We have never been introduced!'

For some inscrutable reason it delighted them both enormously to think that they had never been introduced. . . .

In the later afternoon Lewisham, having unpacked his books to a certain extent and so forth, was visible to all men, visibly in the highest spirits, carrying home Ethel's shopping. There were parcels and cones in blue and parcels in rough grey paper and a bag of confectionery, and out of one of the side pockets of that East-end overcoat the tail of a haddock protruded from its paper. Under such magnificent sanctions and amid such ignoble circumstances did this honeymoon begin.

On Sunday evening they went for a long rambling walk through the quiet streets, coming out at last into Hyde Park. The early spring night was mild and clear and the kindly moonlight was about them. They went to the bridge and looked down the Serpentine, with the lights of Paddington yellow and remote. They stood there, dim little figures and very close together. They whispered and became silent.

Presently it seemed that something passed, and Lewisham began talking in his magnificent vein. He likened the Serpentine to Life, and found Meaning in the dark banks of Kensington Gardens and the remote bright lights. 'The long struggle,' he said, 'and the lights at the end'—though he really did not know what he meant by the lights at the end. Neither did Ethel, though the emotion was indisputable. 'We are Fighting the World,' he said, finding great satisfaction in the thought. 'All the world is against us—and we are fighting it all.'

'We will not be beaten,' said Ethel.

'How could we be beaten—together?' said Lewisham. 'For you I would fight a dozen worlds.'

It seemed a very sweet and noble thing to them under the sympathetic moonlight, almost indeed too easy for their courage to be merely fighting the world.

H. G. WELLS (1866–1946)
Love and Mr. Lewisham, Chaps. 20 and 22

WAITING AT THE KIRK

'Why weep ye by the tide, ladie?
    Why weep ye by the tide?
I'll wed ye to my youngest son,
    And ye shall be his bride:
And ye shall be his bride, ladie,
    Sae comely to be seen'—
But aye she loot the tears down fa'
    For Jock of Hazeldean.

'Now let this wilfu' grief be done,
    And dry that cheek so pale;
Young Frank is chief of Errington
    and lord of Langley-dale;
His step is first in peaceful ha',
    His sword in battle keen'—
But aye she loot the tears down fa'
    For Jock of Hazeldean.

'A chain of gold ye sall not lack,
    Nor braid to bind your hair,
Nor mettled hound, nor managed hawk,
    Nor palfrey fresh and fair;
And you the foremost o' them a'
    Shall ride our forest-queen'—
But aye she loot the tears down fa'
    For Jock of Hazeldean.

The kirk was deck'd at morning-tide,
    The tapers glimmer'd fair;
The priest and bridegroom wait the bride,
    And dame and knight are there:

I

They sought her baith by bower and ha';
The ladie was not seen!
She's o'er the Border, and awa'
Wi' Jock of Hazeldean.

SIR WALTER SCOTT (1771–1832)

MASQUE FOR A MARRIAGE

The Jacobean Court was a scene of elaborate and expensive masquing. The dramatists of Shakespeare's time with their meagre fees for serious and often splendid work (little more than five pounds for the entire rights in a play) resented the huge outlay, sometimes thousands of pounds, on masques at Court. Ben Jonson, who wrote brief scripts for masques, presumably for far more than he could make with a five-act play, dismissed these revels as mere painting and carpentry. But the employment of such talents as those of Inigo Jones ensured that the great sums of money, however large, were spent with taste. The courtiers were the players and must have had considerable proficiency in song and dance and must also have devoted some time to rehearsal, since they had their lines to learn and the movements needed could be complex. The following excerpt is from a Masque 'presented before the King's Majesty at Whitehall on Twelfth Night (1606) in honour of the Lord Hayes and his bride, daughter and heir to the Honourable the Lord Denny, their marriage having been the same day at Court solemnized'. It required intricate devices of scenery presenting a hilly grove, many trees, the bower of Flora, the House of Night, 'artificial bats and owls on wire, continually moving' and 'many other inventions'. The music was provided by

'. . . on the right hand ten musicians, with bass and mean lutes, a bandora, a double sackbut, and an harpischord, with two treble violins; on the other side somewhat nearer the screen were placed nine violins and three lutes, and to answer both the consorts (as it were in a triangle) six cornets, and six chapel voices, were seated almost right against them.'

The Masquers were

1. Lord Walden.
2. Sir Thomas Howard.
3. Sir Henry Carey, Master of the Jewel house.
4. Sir John Preston, Gent. of the K.
5. Sir John Ashley, Privy Chamber.
6. Sir Thomas Jarrett, Pensioner.
7. Sir John Digby, one of the King's Carvers.
8. Sir Thomas Badger, Master of the King's Harriers
9. Master Goringe.

There is no mention of a lady to speak Flora's lines. Perhaps Master Gorringe did that, although women, barred from the public stages, frequently appeared in masques. But here none is mentioned.

The text in this case combined the usual formal style in rhymed verse with the simple dialogue for singing here exemplified. The excerpt is a section of a script that runs to over twenty pages.

Flora

Flowers and good wishes Flora doth present,
Sweet flowers, the ceremonious ornament
Of maiden marriage, Beauty figuring,
And blooming youth; which though we careless fling
About this sacred place, let none profane
Think that these fruits from common hills are ta'en,
Or vulgar vallies which do subject lie
To winter's wrath and cold mortality.
But these are hallowed and immortal flowers
With Flora's hands gathered from Flora's bowers.
Such are her presents, endless as her love,
And such for ever may this night's joy prove.

Zeph

For ever endless may this night's joy prove!
So echoes Zephyrus the friend of Love,
Whose aid Venus implores when she doth bring
Into the naked world the green-leaved spring.
When of the sun's warm beams the nets we weave
That can the stubborn'st heart with love deceive.
That Queen of Beauty and Desire by me
Breathes gently forth this bridal prophecy:
Faithful and fruitful shall these bedmates prove,
Blest in their fortunes, honoured in their love.

Flora

All grace this night, and, Sylvans, so must you,
Off'ring your marriage song with changes new.

THE SONG IN FORM OF A DIALOGUE

Cantor

Who is the happier of the two,
A maid, or wife?

Tenor

Which is more to be desired,
Peace or strife?

Cantor

What strife can be where two are one,
Or what delight to pine alone?

Bass

None such true friends, none so sweet life,
As that between the man and wife.

Tenor

A maid is free, a wife is tied.

Cantor

No maid but fain would be a bride.

Tenor

Why live so many single then?
'Tis not I hope for want of men.

Cantor

The bow and arrow both may fit,
And yet 'tis hard the mark to hit.

Bass

He levels fair that by his side
Lays at night his lovely Bride

Chorus

Sing Io, Hymen! Io, Io, Hymen!

(Stage direction)

This song being ended the whole veil is suddenly drawn,
the grove and trees of gold, and the hill with Diana's tree are
at once discovered.

Night appears in her house with her Nine Hours, apparelled
in large robes of black taffeta, painted thick with stars, their
hairs long, black, and spangled with gold, on their heads
coronets of stars, and their faces black. Every Hour bore in
his hand a black torch, painted with stars, and lighted.

THOMAS CAMPION (1562–1619)
Masque at the Marriage of Lord Hayes

A WEDDING BALLAD

I tell thee, Dick, where I have been,
Where I the rarest things have seen,
   Oh, things without compare!
Such sights again cannot be found
In any place on English ground,
   Be it at wake or fair.

At Charing Cross, hard by the way
Where we (thou know'st) do sell our hay,
   There is a house with stairs;
And there did I see coming down
Such folks as are not in our town,
   Vorty at least, in pairs.

Amongst the rest, one pest'lent fine
(His beard no bigger though than thine)
   Walked on before the rest:
Our landlord looks like nothing to him!
The king (God bless him) 'twould undo him,
   Should he go still so drest.

The maid (and thereby hangs a tale),
For such a maid no Whitsun-Ale
   Could ever yet produce:
No grape that's kindly ripe, could be
So round, so plump, so soft as she,
   Nor half so full of juice.

Her finger was so small, the ring
Would not stay on which they did bring;
   It was too wide a peck:
And to say truth (for out it must)
It looked like the great collar (just)
   About our young colt's neck.

Her feet beneath her petticoat,
Like little mice, stole in and out
  As if they feared the light:
But oh! she dances such a way!
No sun upon an Easter-day
  Is half so fine a sight.

Her cheeks so rare a white was on,
No daisy makes comparison;
  (Who sees them is undone),
For streaks of red were migled there,
Such as are on a Cath'rine pear,
  (The side that's next the sun.)

Just in the nick the cook knocked thrice,
And all the waiters in a trice
  His summons did obey;
Each servingman with dish in hand,
Marched boldly up, like our trained-band,
  Presented, and away.

Now hats fly off, and youths carouse,
Healths first go round and then the House,
  The brides[1] came thick and thick;
And when 'twas named another's health,
Perhaps he made it hers by stealth,
  (And who could help it, Dick?)

O' the sudden up they rise and dance;
Then sit again, and sigh, and glance;
  Then dance again, and kiss:
Thus sev'ral ways the time did pass,
Till ev'ry woman wished her place,
  And ev'ry man wished his.

[1] Toasts to the bride.

By this time all were stol'n aside
To counsel and undress the bride;
   But that he must not know:
But yet 'twas thought he guessed her mind,
And did not mean to stay behind
Above an hour or so.

When in he came (Dick) there she lay
Like new-fal'n snow melting away,
   ('Twas time, I trow, to part:)
Kisses were now the only stay,
Which soon she gave, as who would say,
   Good Boy: with all my heart.

At length the candle's out; and now
All that they had not done, they do:
   What that is, who can tell?
But I believe it was no more
Than thou and I have done before
With Bridget and with Nell.

Sir John Suckling (1609–1642)
Collected Poems
(some stanzas omitted)

WELL, FOR SURE!

Reader, I married him. A quiet wedding we had: he and I, the parson and clerk, were alone present. When we got back from church, I went into the kitchen of the manor-house, where Mary was cooking the dinner and John cleaning the knives, and I said,—

'Mary, I have been married to Mr. Rochester this morning.' The housekeeper and her husband were both of that decent phlegmatic order of people to whom one may at any time safely communicate a remarkable piece of news without incurring the danger of having one's ears pierced by some shrill ejaculation, and subsequently stunned by a torrent of wordy wonderment. Mary did look up, and she did stare at me; the ladle with which she was basting a pair of chickens roasting at the fire, did for some three minutes hang suspended in air; and for the same space of time John's knives also had rest from the polishing process. But Mary, bending again over the roast, said only,—

'Have you, miss? Well, for sure!'

A short time after she pursued—'I seed you go out with the master, but I didn't know you were gone to church to be wed;' and she basted away.

CHARLOTTE BRONTË (1816–1855)
Jane Eyre, Chap. 38

Jane Eyre's progress to matrimony had been long and tortuous. But when her authoress got her to the altar, she set a model of precise statement. What millions of pages would have been saved if there had been more such precise announcements as 'Reader, I married him'.

PART THREE

LATER ON

THE HAPPY HUSBAND

I ha'e a wife o' my ain—
    I'll partake wi' naebody;
I'll tak' cuckold frae nane,
    I'll gi'e cuckold to naebody.
I ha'e a penny to spend,
    There—thanks to naebody;
I ha'e naething to lend—
    I'll borrow frae naebody.

I am naebody's lord—
    I'll be slave to naebody;
I ha'e a guid braid sword,
    I'll tak' dunts[1] frae naebody;
I'll be merry and free,
    I'll be sad for naebody;
If naebody care for me,
    I'll care for naebody.

ROBERT BURNS (1759–1796)
Songs

[1] Blows.

MR. AND MRS. SAMUEL PEPYS

May 11*th*, 1667. My wife being dressed this day in fair hair did make me so mad, that I spoke not one word to her, though I was ready to burst with anger. After that, Creed and I into the Park, and walked, a most pleasant evening, and so took coach, and took up my wife, and in my way home discovered my trouble to my wife for her white locks, swearing several times, which I pray God forgive me for, and bending my fist, that I would not endure it. She, poor wretch, was surprized with it, and made me no answer all the way home; but there we parted, and I to the office late, and then home, and without supper to bed, vexed.

May 12*th* (Lord's day). Up, and to my chamber, to settle some accounts there, and by and by down comes my wife to me in her night-gown, and we begun calmly, that, upon having money to lace her gown for second mourning, she would promise to wear white locks no more in my sight, which I, like a severe fool, thinking not enough, begun to except against, and made her fly out to very high terms and cry, and in her heat, told me of keeping company with Mrs. Knipp, saying, that if I would promise never to see her more—of whom she hath more reason to suspect than I had heretofore of Pembleton —she would never wear white locks more. This vexed me, but I restrained myself from saying any thing, but do think never to see this woman—at least, to have her here more; and so all very good friends as ever.

August 1*st*, 1667. Dined at Sir W. Pen's, only with Mrs. Turner and her husband, on a venison pasty, that stunk like a devil. However, I did not know it till dinner was done. We had nothing but only this, and a leg of mutton, and a pullet or two. Mrs. Markahm was here, with her great belly. I was very merry, and after dinner, upon a motion of the women, I was got to go to the play with them—the first I have seen since before the Dutch's coming upon our coast, and so to the King's house, to see 'The Custome of the Country.' The house mighty empty—more than ever I saw it—and an ill play.

After the play, we went into the house, and spoke with Knipp, who went abroad with us by coach to the Neat Houses, in the way to Chelsy; and there, in a box in a tree,[1] we sat and sang, and talked and eat; my wife out of humour, as she always is, when this woman is by. So, after it was dark, we home. Set Knipp down at home, who told us the story how Nell is gone from the King's house, and is kept by my Lord Buckhurst. Home, the gates of the City shut, it being so late; and at Newgate we find them in trouble, some thieves having this night broke open prison. So we through, and home; and our coachman was fain to drive hard from two or three fellows, which he said were rogues, that he met at the end of Blue-bladder Street, next Cheapside. So set Mrs. Turner home, and then we home, and I to the Office a little; and so home and to bed, my wife in an ill humour still.

December 25*th*, 1668. Christmas Day. To dinner alone with my wife, who poor wretch, sat undressed all day till ten at night, altering and lacing of a noble petticoat; while, by her making the boy read to me the Life of Julius Caesar and Des Cartes' book of Musick.

January 12*th*, 1668–9. This evening I observed my wife mighty dull, and I myself was not mighty fond, because of some hard words she did give me at noon, out of a jealousy at my being abroad this morning which God knows it was upon the business of the Office unexpectedly; but I to bed, not thinking but she would come after me. But waking by and by, out of a slumber, which I usually fall into presently after my coming into the bed, I found she did not prepare, to come to bed, but got fresh candles, and more wood for her fire, it being mighty cold, too. At this being troubled, I after a while prayed her to come to bed; so, after an hour or two, she silent,

---

[1] A summer-house in the branches.

and I now and then praying her to come to bed, she fell out into a fury, that I was a rogue, and false to her. I did, as I might truly, deny it, and was mightily troubled, but all would not serve.

At last, about one o'clock, she came to my side of the bed, and drew my curtaine open, and with the tongs red hot at the ends, made as if she did design to pinch me with them, at which, in dismay, I rose up, and with a few words she laid them down; and did by little and little, very sillily, let all the discourse fall; and about two, but with much seeming difficulty, come to bed, and there lay well all night, and long in bed talking together, with much pleasure, it being, I know, nothing but her doubt of my going out yesterday, without telling her of my going, which did vex her, poor wretch! last night, and I cannot blame her jealousy, though it do vex me to the heart.

SAMUEL PEPYS (1633–1703)
Diary

STRANGERS YET

Strangers yet!
After years of life together,
After fair and stormy weather,
After travel in far lands,
After touch of wedded hands,—
Why thus join'd? Why ever met,
If they must be strangers yet?

Strangers yet!
After childhood's winning ways,
After care and blame and praise,
Counsel ask'd and wisdom given,
After mutual prayers to Heaven,
Child and parent scarce regret
When they part—are strangers yet.

Strangers yet!
After strife for common ends—
After title of 'old friends,'
After passions fierce and tender,
After cheerful self-surrender,
Hearts may beat and eyes be met,
And the souls be strangers yet.

Strangers yet!
Oh! the bitter thought to scan
All the loneliness of man:—
Nature, by magnetic laws,
Circle unto circle draws,
But they only touch when met,
Never mingle—strangers yet.

R. M. (Milnes) Lord Houghton
(1809–1885)
Poems

K

COLLINGWOOD TO HIS WIFE SARAH

—•◦◦◦❀◦◦◦•—

Admiral Collingwood commanded the *Royal Sovereign* at Trafalgar and took over supreme command of the Fleet on Nelson's death.

Ocean, June 16, 1806

THIS DAY MY LOVE, is the anniversary of our marriage, and I wish you many happy returns of it. If ever we have peace, I hope to spend my latter days amid my family, which is the only sort of happiness I can enjoy. After this life of labour, to retire to peace and quietness is all I look for in the world. Should we decide to change the place of our dwelling, our route would of course be to the southward of Morpeth: but then I should be forever regretting those beautiful views, which are no where to be exceeded; and even the rattling of that old wagon that used to pass our door at 6 o'clock in a Winter's morning had its charms. The fact is, whenever I think how I am to be happy again, my thoughts carry me back to Morpeth, where, out of the fuss and parade of the world, surrounded by those I loved most dearly and who loved me, I enjoyed as much happiness as my nature is capable of. Many things that I see in the world give me a distaste to the finery of it. The great knaves are not like those poor unfortunates, who, driven perhaps to distress from accidents which they could not prevent or at least not educated in principles of honour and honesty, are hanged for some little thievery; while a knave of education and high breeding, who brandishes his honour in the eyes of the world, would rob a state to its ruin. For the first, I feel pity and compassion; for the latter, abhorrence and contempt: they are tenfold vicious.

Have you read—but what I am more interested about, is your sister with you, and is she well and happy? Tell her—God bless her!—I wish I were with you, that we might have a good laugh. God bless me! I have scarcely laughed these three years. I am here, with a very reduced force, having been obliged to make detachments to all quarters. This leaves me weak, while the Spaniards and French within are daily gaining strength. They have patched and pieced until they have now a very considerable fleet. Whether they will venture out I do not know: if they come, I have no doubt we shall do an excellent deed, and then I will bring them to England myself.

How do the dear girls go on? I would have them taught geometry, which is of all sciences in the world the most entertaining: it expands the mind more to the knowledge of all things in nature, and better teaches to distinguish between truths and such things as have the appearance of being truths, yet are not, than any other. Their education and the proper cultivation of the sense which God has given them, are the objects on which my happiness most depends. To inspire them with a love of every thing that is honourable and virtuous, though in rags, and with comtempt for vanity in embroidery, is the way to make them the darlings of my heart. They should not only read, but it requires a careful selection of books; nor should they ever have access to two at the same time: but when a subject is begun, it should be finished before anything else is undertaken. How would it enlarge their minds, if they could acquire a sufficient knowledge of mathematics and astronomy to give them an idea of the beauty and wonders of the creation! I am persuaded that the generality of people, and particularly fine ladies, only adore God because they are told it is proper and the fashion to go to Church; but I would have my girls gain such knowledge of the works of creation, that they may have a fixed idea of the nature of that Being who could be the author of such a world. Whenever they have that, nothing on this side of the moon will give them much uneasiness of mind. I do not mean that they should be Stoics, or want the common feelings for the sufferings that flesh is heir to; but they would then have a source of consolation for the worst that could happen.

Tell me how do the trees which I planted thrive? Is there shade under the three oaks for a comfortable summer seat? Do the poplars grow at the walk, and does the wall of terrace stand firm? My bankers tell me that all my money in their hands is exhausted by fees on the peerage, and that I am in their debt, which is a new epoch in my life, for it is the first time I was ever in debt since I was a Midshipman. Here I get nothing; but then my expenses are nothing, and I do not want it, particularly now that I have got my knives, forks, teapot, and the things you were so kind as to send me.

Admiral LORD COLLINGWOOD (1750–1810)
Letters

TAMBURLAINE MADE WIDOWER

The bellicose, world-conquering Tamburlaine, turned by Marlowe into a master of rhetorical poetry, was devoted to his Egyptian wife and empress, Zenocrate, and made the heavens ring and other nations bleed for her death after a seizure.

The arras is drawn, and Zenocrate is discovered lying in her bed of state; Tamburlaine sitting by her; three Physicians about her bed, tempering potions; her three sons, Calyphas, Amyras, and Celebinus; Theridamas, Techelles and Usumcasane.

Tamburlaine. Black is the beauty of the brightest day;
    The golden ball of heaven's eternal fire,
    That danc'd with glory on the silver waves,
    Now wants the fuel that inflam'd his beams;
    And all with faintness, and for foul disgrace,
    He binds his temples with a frowning cloud,
    Ready to darken earth with endless night.
    Zenocrate, that gave him light and life,
    Whose eyes shot fire from their ivory brows,
    And temper'd every soul with lively heat,
    Now by the malice of the angry skies,
    Whose jealousy admits no second mate,
    Draws in the comfort of her latest breath,
    All dazzled with the hellish mists of death.
    Now walk the angels on the walls of heaven,
    As sentinels to warn th' immortal souls
    To entertain divine Zenocrate:
    Apollo, Cynthia, and the ceaseless lamps
    That gently look'd upon this loathsome earth,
    Shine downwards now no more, but deck the heavens
    To entertain divine Zenocrate:
    The crystal springs, whose taste illuminates
    Refined eyes with an eternal sight,

Like tried silver run through Paradise
To entertain divine Zenocrate:
The cherubins and holy seraphins,
That sing and play before the King of Kings,
Use all their voices and their instruments
To entertain divine Zenocrate;
And, in this sweet and curious harmony,
The god that tunes this music to our souls
Holds out his hand in highest majesty
To entertain divine Zenocrate.

*

Live still, my love, and so conserve my life,
Or, dying, be the author of my death.

Zenocrate. Live still, my lord; O, let my sovereign live!
But let me die, my love, yes, let me die;
With love and patience let your true love die:
Your grief and fury hurts my second life.
Yet let me kiss my lord before I die,
And let me die with kissing of my lord.
But, since my life is lengthen'd yet a while,
Let me take leave of these my loving sons,
And of my lords, whose true nobility
Have merited my latest memory.
Sweet sons, farewell! in death resemble me,
And in your lives your father's excellence.
Some music, and my fit will cease, my lord.

They call for music.

Tamburlaine. Proud fury, and intolerable fit,
That dares torment the body of my love,
And scourge the scourge of the immortal God!
Now are those spheres, where Cupid us'd to sit,
Wounding the world with wonder and with love,
Sadly supplied with pale and ghastly death,
Whose darts do pierce the centre of my soul.
Her sacred beauty hath enchanted heaven;

And, had she liv'd before the siege of Troy,
Helen, whose beauty summon'd Greece to arms,
And drew a thousand ships to Tenedos,
Had not been nam'd in Homer's Iliads,—
Her name had been in every line he wrote;
Or, had those wanton poets, for whose birth
Old Rome was proud, but gaz'd a while on her,
Nor Lesbia nor Corinna had been nam'd,—
Zenocrate had been the argument
Of every epigram or elegy.

> *The music sounds—Zenocrate dies.*

What, is she dead? Techelles, draw thy sword,
And wound the earth, that it may cleave in twain,
And we descend into th' infernal vaults,
To hale the Fatal Sisters by the hair,
And throw them in the triple moat of hell,
For taking hence my fair Zenocrate.
Casane and Theridamas, to arms!
Raise cavalieros higher than the clouds,
And with the cannon break the frame of heaven;
Batter the shining palace of the sun,
And shiver all the starry firmament,
For amorous Jove hath snatch'd my love from hence,
Meaning to make her stately queen of heaven.

*

Theridamas. Ah, good my lord, be patient! she is dead,
And all this raging cannot make her live.
If words might serve, our voice hath rent the air;
If tears, our eyes have water'd all the earth;
If grief, our murder'd hearts have strained forth blood:
Nothing prevails, for she is dead, my lord.

Tamburlaine. For she is dead! thy words do pierce my soul:
Ah, sweet Theridamas, say so no more!
Though she be dead, yet let me think she lives,
And feed my mind what dies for want of her.

Where'er her soul be, thou (*to the body*) shalt stay with me.
Embalm'd with cassia, ambergris, and myrrh,
Not lapt in lead, but in a sheet of gold,
And, till I die, thou shalt not be interr'd.
Then in as rich a tomb as Mausolus'
We both will rest, and have one epitaph
Writ in as many several languages
As I have conquer'd kingdoms with my sword.
This cursed town will I consume with fire,
Because this place bereft me of my love;
The houses, burnt, will look as if they mourn'd;
And here will I set up her stature
And march about it with my mourning camp,
Drooping and pining for Zenocrate.

The arras is drawn.

CHRISTOPHER MARLOWE (1564–1593)
The Second Part of *Tamburlaine the Great*,
Act II, Scene IV

NO REST FOR A GOOD WIFE

Who can find a virtuous woman? for her price is far above
rubies.

The heart of her husband doth safely trust in her, so that he
shall have no need of spoil.

She will do him good and not evil all the days of her life.

She seeketh wool, and flax, and worketh willingly with her
hands.

She is like the merchants' ships; she bringeth her food from
afar.

She riseth also while it is yet night, and giveth meat to her
household, and a portion to her maidens.

She considereth a field, and buyeth it: with the fruit of her
hands she planteth a vineyard.

She girdeth her loins with strength, and strengtheneth her arms.

She perceiveth that her merchandise is good: her candle goeth
not out by night.

She layeth her hands to the spindle, and her hands hold the
distaff.

She stretcheth out her hand to the poor; yea, she reacheth forth
her hands to the needy.

She is not afraid of the snow for her household: for all her
household are clothed with scarlet.

She maketh herself coverings of tapestry; her clothing is silk
and purple.

Her husband is known in the gates, when he sitteth among the
elders of the land.

She maketh fine linen, and selleth it; and delivereth girdles
unto the merchant.

Strength and honour are her clothing; and she shall rejoice in
time to come.

She openeth her mouth with wisdom; and in her tongue is the
law of kindness.

She looketh well to the ways of her household, and eateth not
the bread of idleness.

Her children arise up, and call her blessed; her husband also,
and he praiseth her.

Many daughters have done virtuously, but thou excellest
them all.

Favour is deceitful, and beauty is vain: but a woman that
feareth the Lord, she shall be praised.

Give her of the fruit of her hands; and let her own works
praise her in the gates.

The Holy Bible
Authorized Version, 1611
The Book of Proverbs, Chap. 31

A SOVEREIGN CLAIM

That brilliant soldier and martyr to his beliefs, the Marquis of Montrose, married Magdalen Carnegie. In Miss Veronica Wedgwood's words 'she withdrew more and more from her husband's friends into the secure shelter of her cautiously time-serving family'. Hence the reference to 'a Synod in thine heart' and his appeal for loyalty in the adventures which she feared.

My dear and only Love, I pray,
That little world of thee
Be governed by no other sway
Than purest monarchy.
For if confusion have a part,
Which virtuous souls abhor,
And hold a Synod in thine heart,
I'll never love thee more.

Like Alexander I will reign,
And I will reign alone;
My thoughts did ever more disdain
A rival on my throne.
He either fears his fate too much,
Or his deserts are small,
That dares not put it to the touch,
To gain or lose it all.

And in the Empire of thine heart,
Where I should solely be,
If others do pretend a part
Or dare to vie with me,
Or Committees if thou erect
And go on such a score,
I'll laugh and sing at thy neglect,
And never love thee more.

But if thou wilt prove faithful then,
And constant of thy word,
I'll make thee glorious by my pen
And famous by my sword.
I'll serve thee in such noble ways
Was never heard before;
I'll crown and deck thee all with bays
And love thee more and more.

JAMES GRAHAM, Marquis of Montrose
(1612–1650)

EPITAPH

In bliss is hee,
  Whom I lov'd best,
Thrice happy shee
  With him to rest.

So shall I bee
  With him I loved,
And hee with mee,
  And both us blessed.

Love made me Poet,
  And this I writt,
My heart did do yt
  And not my wit.

A N O N (in Burford Churchyard)

A MUCH-MARRIED MINISTER

John Galt, the Scottish author who was also a gallant but ill-rewarded pioneer of settlements in Canada, has been much over-shadowed by the popularity and renown of his great contemporary Sir Walter Scott that the excellence of his writing has not been sufficiently remembered. *Annals of the Parish*, published in 1821, are the recollections of Mr. Balwhidder, an imagined minister in an Ayrshire village called Dalmailing, where he was 'placed and settled' in 1760, a year after the birth of Robert Burns near by. The picture of South West Scotland in the time of Burns and just before the impact of the Industrial Revolution is most amusing as well as most useful to the social historian. Mr. Balwhidder, it will be seen, did not favour the celibacy of the clergy.

Upon the subject of taking my cousin, Miss Betty Lanshaw, for my first wife, I have little to say.—It was more out of a compassionate habitual affection, than the passion of love. We were brought up by our grandmother in the same house, and it was a thing spoken of from the beginning, that Betty and me were to be married. So, when she heard that the Laird of Breadland had given me the presentation of Dalmailing, she began to prepare for the wedding; and as soon as the placing was well over, and the manse in order, I gaed to Ayr, where she was, and we were quietly married, and came home in a chaise, bringing with us her little brother Andrew, that died in the East Indies, and he lived and was brought up by us.

Now, this is all, I think that happened in that year worthy of being mentioned, except that at the sacrament, when old Mr. Kilfuddy was preaching in the tent, it came on such a thunder-plump, that there was not a single soul stayed in the kirkyard to hear him; for the which he was greatly mortified, and never after came to our preachings.

Three years later a disastrous fire at a linen-mill destroyed much of the year's crop of lint in the parish.

The first Mrs. Balwhidder lost upwards of twelve stone (of lint) which we had raised on the glebe with no small pains,

watering it in the drouth, as it was intended for sarking[1] to ourselves, and sheets and napery. A great loss indeed it was, and
the vexation thereof had a visible effect on Mrs. Balwhidder's
health, which from the spring had been in a dwining way. But
for it, I think she might have wrestled through the winter:
however, it was ordered otherwise, and she was removed from
mine to Abraham's bosom on Christmas-day, and buried on
Hogmany, for it was thought uncanny to have a dead corpse in
the house on the new-year's day.

After an interval of two years Mr. Balwhidder married again.

I had placed my affections, with due consideration, on Miss
Lizy Kibbock, the well brought-up daughter of Mr. Joseph
Kibbock of the Gorbyholm, who was the first that made a
speculation in the farming way in Ayrshire, and whose cheese
were of such an excellent quality, that they have, under the
name of Delap-cheese, spread far and wide over the civilized
world. Miss Lizy and me were married on the 29th day of
April, with some inconvenience to both sides, on account of the
dread that we had of being married in May; for it is said—

> 'Of the marriages in May,
> The bairns die of a decay.'

However, married we were, and we hired the Irville chaise, and
with Miss Jenny her sister, and Becky Cairns her niece, who
sat on a portmanty at our feet, we went on a pleasure jaunt to
Glasgow, where we bought a miracle of useful things for the
manse, that neither the first Mrs. Balwhidder nor me ever
thought of; but the second Mrs. Balwhidder that was, had a
geni for management, and it was extraordinary what she could
go through. Well may I speak of her with commendations; for
she was the bee that made my honey, although at first things
did not go so clear with us. For she found the manse rookit[2] and
herrit[3], and there was such a supply of plenishing of all sort
wanted, that I thought myself ruined and undone by her care

---

[1] Making shirts.   [2] Deprived.   [3] Plundered.

and industry. There was such a buying of wool to make blankets, with a booming of the meikle wheel to spin the same, and such birring of the little wheel for sheets and napery, that the manse was for many a day like an organ kist. Then we had milk cows, and the calves to bring up, and a kirning of butter, and a making of cheese; in short, I was almost by myself with the jangle and din, which prevented me from writing a book as I had proposed, and I for a time thought of the peaceful and kindly nature of the first Mrs. Balwhidder with a sigh; but the outcoming was soon manifest. The second Mrs. Balwhidder sent her butter on the market-days to Irville, and her cheese from time to time to Glasgow, to Mrs. Firlot, that kept the huxtry in the Saltmarket; and they were both so well made, that our dairy was just a coining of money, insomuch that, after the first year, we had the whole tot of my stipend to put untouched into the bank.

But I must say, that although we were thus making siller like sclate[1] stones, I was not satisfied in my own mind that I had got the manse merely to be a factory of butter and cheese, and to breed up veal calves for the slaughter; so I spoke to the second Mrs. Balwhidder, and pointed out to her what I thought the error of our way; but she had been so ingrained with the profitable management of cows and grumphies[2] in her father's house, that she could not desist, at the which I was greatly grieved. By-and-by, however, I began to discern that there was something as good in her example as the giving of alms to the poor folk; for all the wives of the parish were stirred up by it into a wonderful thrift, and nothing was heard of in every house, but of quiltings and wabs to weave; insomuch that, before many years came round, there was not a better stocked parish, with blankets and napery, than mine was, within the bounds of Scotland.

The second Mrs. Balwhidder died in 1796.

In the month of February my second wife was gathered to the Lord. She had been very ill for some time with an income

---

[1] Slate.   [2] Sows.

in her side, which no medicine could remove. I had the best doctors in the country-side to her; but their skill was of no avail, their opinions being that her ail was caused by an internal abscess, for which physic has provided no cure. Her death was to me a great sorrow; for she was a most excellent wife, industrious to a degree, and managed every thing with so brisk a hand, that nothing went wrong that she put it to. With her I had grown richer than any other minister in the presby-tery; but, above all, she was the mother of my bairns, which gave her a double claim upon me.

I laid her by the side of my first love, Betty Lanshaw, my own cousin that was, and I inscribed her name upon the same headstone; but time had drained my poetical vein, and I have not yet been able to indite an epitaph on her merits and virtues, for she had an eminent share of both. Her greatest fault—the best have their faults—was an over-earnestness to gather gear; in the doing of which I thought she sometimes sacrificed the comforts of a pleasant fireside; for she was never in her element but when she was keeping the servants eident[1] at their work. But, if by this she subtracted something from the quietude that was most consonant to my nature, she has left cause, both in bank and bond, for me and her bairns to bless her great household activity.

She was not long deposited in her place of rest till I had occasion to find her loss. All my things were kept by her in a most perjink[2] and excellent order; but they soon fell into an amazing confusion; for, as she often said to me, I had a turn for heedlessness; insomuch, that although my daughter Janet was grown up, and able to keep the house, I saw that it would be necessary, as soon as decency would allow, for me to take another wife. I was moved to this chiefly by foreseeing that my daughter would in time be married, and taken away from me, but more on account of the servant lasses, who grew out of all bounds, verifying the proverb, 'Well kens the mouse when the cat's out of the house'. Besides this, I was now far down in the vale of years, and could not expect to be long without

---

[1] Busy.   [2] Precise.

L

feeling some of the penalties of old age, although I was still a hail and sound man. It therefore behoved me to look in time for a help-mate, to tend me in approaching infirmities.

Accordingly, I bent my brows, and looked towards Irville, which is an abundant trone for widows and other single women; and I fixed my purpose on Mrs. Nugent, the relic of a professor in the university of Glasgow, both because she was a well-bred woman, without any children to plea about the interest of my own two, and likewise because she was held in great estimation by all who knew her, as a lady of a Christian principle.

It was some time in the summer, however, before I made up my mind to speak to her on the subject; but one afternoon, in the month of August, I resolved to do so, and with that intent walked leisurely over to Irville; and after calling on the Rev. Dr. Dinwiddie, the minister, I stepped in, as if by chance, to Mrs. Nugent's. I could see that she was a little surprised at my visit; however, she treated me with every possible civility, and her servant lass bringing in the tea-things in a most orderly manner, as punctually as the clock was striking, she invited me to sit still, and drink my tea with her; which I did, being none displeased to get such encouragement. However, I said nothing that time, but returned to the manse, very well content with what I had observed, which made me fain to repeat my visit. So, in the course of the week, taking Janet my daughter with me, we walked over in the forenoon, and called at Mrs. Nugent's first, before going to any other house; and Janet saying, as we came out to go to the minister's, that she thought Mrs. Nugent an agreeable woman, I determined to knock the nail on the head without further delay.

Accordingly, I invited the minister and his wife to dine with us on the Thursday following; and before leaving the town, I made Janet, while the minister and me were handling a subject, as a sort of thing of common civility, go to Mrs. Nugent, and invite her also. Dr. Dinwiddie was a gleg[1] man, of a jocose nature; and he, guessing something of what I was

[1] Clever and lively.

ettling[1] at, was very mirthful with me; but I kept my own counsel till a meet season.

On the Thursday, the company as invited came, and nothing extraordinary was seen; but in cutting up and helping a hen, Dr. Dinwiddie put one wing on Mrs. Nugent's plate, and the other wing on my plate, and said, there have been greater miracles than these two wings flying together, which was a sharp joke, that caused no little merriment at the expense of Mrs. Nugent and me. I, however, to show that I was none daunted, laid a leg also on her plate, and took another on my own, saying, in the words of the reverend doctor, there have been greater miracles than that these two legs should lie in the same nest, which was thought a very clever come off; and, at the same time, I gave Mrs. Nugent a kindly nip on her sonsy arm, which was breaking the ice in as pleasant a way as could be. In short, before anything passed between ourselves on the subject, we were set down for a trysted pair; and this being the case, we were married as soon as a twelvemonth and a day had passed from the death of the second Mrs. Balwhidder; and neither of us have had occasion to rue the bargain.

JOHN GALT (1779–1839)
Annals of the Parish

[1] Aiming.

CAPRICIOUS TULIPS

Papillia, wedded to her am'rous spark,
Sighs for the shades—'How charming is a Park!'
A Park is purchas'd, but the Fair he sees
All bath'd in tears—'Oh odious, odious Trees!'
Ladies, like variegated Tulips, show;
'Tis to their Changes half their charms we owe.

ALEXANDER POPE (1688–1744)
Epistle to a Lady

AN ENGLISHMAN'S HOME

————•◦◦◦❀◦◦◦•————

Why should I not publish my diary? I have often seen reminiscences of people I have never even heard of, and I fail to see—because I do not happen to be a 'Somebody'—why my diary should not be interesting. My only regret is that I did not commence it when I was a youth.

Charles Pooter

The Laurels,
  Brickfield Terrace,
    Holloway.

My dear wife Carrie and I have just been a week in our new house, 'The Laurels', Brickfield Terrace, Holloway—a nice six-roomed residence, not counting basement, with a front breakfast-parlour. We have a little front garden; and there is a flight of ten steps up to the front door, which, by-the-by, we keep locked with the chain up. Cummings, Gowing, and our other intimate friends always come to the side entrance, which saves the servant the trouble of going up to the front door, thereby taking her from her work. We have a nice little back garden which runs down to the railway. We were rather afraid of the noise of the trains at first, but the landlord said we should not notice them after a bit, and took £2 off the rent. He was certainly right; and beyond the cracking of the garden wall at the bottom, we have suffered no inconvenience.

After my work in the City, I like to be at home. What's the good of a home, if you are never in it? 'Home, Sweet Home', that's my motto. I am always in of an evening. Our old friend Gowing may drop in without ceremony; so may Cummings, who lives opposite. My dear wife Caroline and I are pleased to see them, if they like to drop in on us. But Carrie and I can manage to pass our evenings together without friends. There is always something to be done: a tin-tack here, a Venetian blind to put straight, a fan to nail up, or part of a carpet to nail down—all of which I can do with my pipe in my mouth; while Carrie is not above putting a button on a shirt, mending a pillow-case, or practising the 'Sylvia Gavotte' on our new cottage piano (on the three years' system), manufactured by W. Bilkson (in small letters), from Collard and Collard (in very large letters). It is also a great comfort to us to know that our boy Willie is getting on so well in the Bank at Oldham. We should like to see more of him. Now for my diary:

April 12. In the evening, after tea, Gowing dropped in, and we had a smoke together in the breakfast-parlour. Carrie joined us later, but did not stay long, saying the smoke was too much for her. It was also rather too much for me, for Gowing had given me what he called a green cigar, one that his friend Shoemach had just brought over from America. The cigar didn't look green, but I fancy I must have done so; for when I had smoked a little more than half I was obliged to retire on the pretext of telling Sarah to bring in the glasses.

I took a walk round the garden three or four times, feeling the need of fresh air. On returning Gowing noticed I was not smoking: offered me another cigar, which I politely declined. Gowing began his usual sniffling, so, anticipating him, I said: 'You're not going to complain of the smell of paint again?' He said: 'No, not this time; but I'll tell you what, I distinctly smell dry rot.' I don't often make jokes but I replied: 'You're talking a lot of *dry rot* yourself.' I could not help roaring at this, and Carrie said her sides quite ached with laughter. I never was so immensely tickled by anything I had ever said before. I actually woke up twice during the night, and laughed till the bed shook.

April 13. An extraordinary coincidence: Carrie had called in a woman to make some chintz covers for our drawing-room chairs and sofa to prevent the sun fading the green rep of the furniture. I saw the woman, and recognized her as a woman who used to work years ago for my old aunt at Clapham. It only shows how small the world is.

April 14. Spent the whole of the afternoon in the garden, having this morning picked up at a bookstall for fivepence a capital little book, in good condition, on Gardening. I procured and sowed some half-hardy annuals in what I fancy will be a warm, sunny border. I thought of a joke, and called out Carrie. Carrie came out rather testy, I thought. I said: 'I have just discovered we have got a lodging-house.' She replied: 'How do you mean?' I said: 'Look at the *boarders.*' Carrie said: 'Is that all you wanted me for?' I said: 'Any other time you would have laughed at my little pleasantry.' Carrie said: 'Certainly—*at any other time*, but not when I am busy in the house.' The stairs look very nice. Gowing called, and said the stairs looked *all right*, but it made the banisters look *all wrong*, and suggested a coat of paint on them also, which Carrie quite agreed with. I walked round to Putley, and fortunately he was out, so I had a good excuse to let the banisters slide. By-the-by, that is rather funny.

GEORGE GROSSMITH (1847–1912)
WEEDON GROSSMITH (1854–1919)
The Diary of a Nobody, from Chaps. 1 and 2

THE HERDSMAN'S WIFE

Ah, what is love? It is a pretty thing.
As sweet unto a shepherd as a king;
   And sweeter too;
For kings have cares that wait upon a crown,
And cares can make the sweetest love frown:
   Ah then, ah then.
If country loves such sweet desires do gain,
What lady would not love a shepherd swain?

His flocks are folded, he comes home at night,
As merry as a king in his delight;
   A merrier too;
For kings bethink them what the state require,
Where shepherds careless carol by the fire:
   Ah then, ah then.
If country loves such sweet desires do gain,
What lady would not love a shepherd swain?

He kisseth first, then sits as blithe to eat
His cream and curds as doth the king his meat;
   And blither too;
For kings have often fears when they do sup,
Where shepherds dread no poison in their cup:
   Ah then, ah then.
If country loves such sweet desires do gain,
What lady would not love a shepherd swain?

Upon his couch of straw he sleeps as sound,
As doth the king upon his beds of down,
   More sounder too;
For cares cause kings full oft their sleep to spill,[1]

[1] Lose.

Where weary shepherds lie and snort their fill:
   Ah then, ah then.
If country loves such sweet desires do gain,
What lady would not love a shepherd swain?

Thus with his wife he spends the year as blithe
As doth the king at every tide or sithe;[1]
   And blither too;
For kings have wars and broils to take in hand,
Where shepherds laugh and love upon the land;
   Ah then, ah then.
If country loves such sweet desires do gain,
What lady would not love a shepherd swain?

ROBERT GREENE (1560?–1592)
Songs from *Mourning Garment*

[1] Time.

POLES APART

Mrs. Sullen. How long have we been married?

Squire Sullen. By the almanac, fourteen months; but by my account fourteen years.

Mrs. Sullen. 'Tis thereabouts by my reckoning. Pray, spouse, what did you marry for?

Squire Sullen. To get an heir to my estate.

Sir Charles. And have you succeeded?

Squire Sullen. No.

Archer. The condition fails on his side.—Pray, madam, what did you marry for?

Mrs. Sullen. To support the weakness of my sex by the strength of his, and to enjoy the pleasures of an agreeable society.

Sir Charles. Are your expectations answered?

Mrs. Sullen. No.

Sir Charles. What are the bars to your mutual contentment?

Mrs. Sullen. In the first place, I can't drink ale with him.

Squire Sullen. Nor can I drink tea with her.

Mrs. Sullen. I can't hunt with you.

Squire Sullen. Nor can I dance with you.

Mrs. Sullen. I hate cocking and racing.

Squire Sullen. And I abhor ombre and piquet.

Mrs. Sullen. Your silence is intolerable.

Squire Sullen. Your prating is worse.

Mrs. Sullen. Have we not been a perpetual offence to each other? a gnawing vulture at the heart?

Squire Sullen. A frightful goblin to the sight.

Mrs. Sullen. A porcupine to the feeling.

Squire Sullen. Perpetual wormwood to the taste.

Mrs. Sullen. Is there on earth a thing we could agree in?

Squire Sullen. Yes—to part.

Mrs. Sullen. With all my heart.

Squire Sullen. Your hand.

Mrs. Sullen. Here.

Squire Sullen. These hands joined us, these shall part.—Away!

Mrs. Sullen. North.

Squire Sullen. South.

Mrs. Sullen. East.

Squire Sullen. West—far as the poles asunder.

GEORGE FARQUHAR (1678–1707)
The Beaux' Stratagem, Act V, Scene 4

WIFE LOST, WIFE GAINED

I play'd with you 'mid cowslips blowing,
    When I was six and you were four;
When garlands weaving, flower-balls throwing,
    Were pleasures soon to please no more.
Through groves and meads, o'er grass and heather,
    With little playmates, to and fro,
We wander'd hand in hand together;
    But that was sixty years ago.

You grew a lovely roseate maiden,
    And still our early love was strong;
Still with no care our days were laden,
    They glided joyously along;
And I did love you very early,
    How dearly words want power to show;
I thought your heart was touched as nearly;
    But that was fifty years ago.

The other lovers came around you,
    Your beauty grew from year to year,
And many a splendid circle found you
    The centre of its glittering sphere.
I saw you then, first vows forsaking,
    On rank and wealth your hand bestow;
O, then I thought my heart was breaking!—
    But that was forty years ago.

And I lived on, to wed another;
    No cause she gave me to repine;
And when I heard you were a mother,
    I did not wish the children mine.

My own young flock, in fair progression,
 Made up a pleasant Christmas row:
My joy in them was past expression;
 But that was thirty years ago.

You grew a matron plump and comely,
 You dwelt in fashion's brightest blaze;
My earthly lot was far more homely:
 But I too had my festal days.
No merrier eyes have ever glisten'd
 Around the hearth-stone's wintry glow,
Than when my youngest child was christen'd;
 But that was twenty years ago.

Time pass'd. My eldest girl was married,
 And I am now a grandsire gray;
One pet of four years old I've carried
 Among the wild-flowered meads to play.
In our old fields of childish pleasure,
 Where now, as then, the cowslips blow,
She fills her basket's ample measure;
 And that is not ten years ago.

But though first love's impassion'd blindness
 Has pass'd away in colder light,
I still have thought of you with kindness,
 And shall do, till our last good-night.
The ever-rolling silent hours
 Will bring a time we shall not know,
When our young days of gathering flowers
 Will be a hundred years ago.

THOMAS LOVE PEACOCK (1785-1866)
Poem, Love and Age

NO ARGUMENT WANTED

The Earl of Surrey's tranquil ambition for a life 'without debate' was not realized. He was tried for high treason at the command of Henry VIII, unjustly condemned, and executed on Tower Hill before he was thirty.

Martial, the things that do attain
The happy life, be these, I find:
The riches left, not got with pain;
The fruitful ground, the quiet mind:

The equal friend, no grudge, no strife;
No charge of rule, nor governance;
Without disease, the healthful life;
The household of continuance:

The mean diet, no delicate fare;
True wisdom join'd with simpleness;
The night dischargéd of all care,
Where wine the wit may not oppress:

The faithful wife, without debate;
Such sleeps as may beguile the night:
Contented with thine own estate;
No wish for death, ne fear his might.

HENRY HOWARD, EARL OF SURREY (1518–1547)
Poems

PENN OF PENNSYLVANIA

William Penn, banished from Oxford because of his religious non-conformity and later sent to the Tower for his Quaker faith, inherited money from his father which he was allowed to exchange for a grant of land in North America. He was thus able to found the colony of Pennsylvania where he provided a refuge for his fellow-victims of religious persecution. Before one of his voyages he wrote this letter to his family. Students of the English language may be interested to note that 'on the square', which seems to us colloquial, was an old usage and employed by one who wrote gravely and with no intention to deal in slang.

Worminghurst, 4th of the 6th Month, 1682

My dear Wife and Children,

My love, which neither sea, nor land, nor death can extinguish towards you, most endearedly visits you with eternal embraces, and will abide with you for ever. My dear wife, remember thou wast the love of my youth and the joy of my life, the most beloved, as well as most worthy of all my earthly comforts. God knows and thou knowest it, it was a match of Providence's own making. Now I am to leave thee, and that without knowing whether I shall ever see thee more in this life.

Take my counsel to thy bosom:—

Firstly. Let the fear of the Lord dwell in you richly.

Secondly. Be diligent in meetings and worship and business, and let meetings be kept once a day in the family, and, my dearest, divide thy time and be regular. In the morning, view the business of the house. Grieve not thyself with careless servants, they will disorder thee, rather pay them and let them go. It is best to avoid many words, which I know wound the soul.

Thirdly. Cast up thy income and see what it daily amounts to, and I beseech thee live low and sparingly until my debts are paid. I write not as doubtful of thee, but to quicken thee.

Fourthly. My dearest, let me recommend to thy care the dear children abundantly beloved of me. Breed them up in the love of virtue. I had rather they were homely than finely bred. Religion in the heart leads into true civility, teaching men and women to be mild and courteous.

Fifthly. Breed them up in a love one of another. Tell them it is the charge I left behind me. Tell them it was my counsel, they should be tender and affectionate one to another. For their learning be liberal, spare no cost. Rather keep an ingenuous person in the house to teach them, than send them to schools, too many evil impressions being commonly received there. And now, dear children, be obedient to your dear mother, whose virtue and good name is an honour to you, for she hath been exceeded by none in integrity, industry, and virtue, and good understanding, qualities not usual among women of her worldly condition and quality. Be temperate in all things, watch against anger, and avoid flatterers, who are thieves in disguise. Be plain in your apparel, let your virtue be your ornament. Be not busy-bodies, meddle not with other folk's manners, and for you who are likely to be concerned in the Government of Pennsylvania, especially my first born, be lowly, diligent and tender. Keep upon the square, for God sees you. Use no tricks, but let your heart be upright before the Lord. So may my God, who hath blessed me with abundant mercies, guide you by His counsel, bless you, and bring you to His eternal glory. So farewell to my thrice beloved wife and children.

Yours as God pleaseth, which no waters can quench, no time forget, nor distance wear away, but remains for ever.

WILLIAM PENN

SUSAN AND THE SAILOR

All in the Downs the fleet was moor'd,
  The streamers waving in the wind,
When black-eyed Susan came aboard;
  'O! where shall I my true-love find?
Tell me, ye jovial sailors, tell me true
If my sweet William sails among the crew,'

William, who high upon the yard
  Rock'd with the billow to and fro,
Soon as her well-known voice he heard
  He sigh'd, and cast his eyes below:
The cord slides swiftly through his glowing hands,
And quick as lightning on the deck he stands.

So the sweet lark, high poised in air,
  Shuts close his pinions to his breast
If chance his mate's shrill call he hear,
  And drops at once into her nest:—
The noblest captain in the British fleet
Might envy William's lip those kisses sweet.

'O Susan, Susan, lovely dear,
  My vows shall ever true remain;
Let me kiss off that falling tear;
  We only part to meet again,
Change as ye list, ye winds; my heart shall be
The faithful compass that still points to thee.

'Believe not what the landmen say
  Who tempt with doubts thy constant mind:
They'll tell thee, sailors, when away,
  In every port a mistress find:
Yes, yes, believe them when they tell thee so,
For Thou art present wheresoe'er I go.

M

'If so fair India's coast we sail,
  Thy eyes are seen in diamonds bright,
Thy breath is Afric's spicy gale,
  Thy skin is ivory so white,
Thus every beauteous object that I view
Wakes in my soul some charm of lovely Sue.

'Though battle call me from thy arms
  Let not my pretty Susan mourn;
Though cannon roar, yet safe from harms
  William shall to his Dear return.
Love turns aside the balls that round me fly,
Lest precious tears should drop from Susan's eye.'

The boatswain gave the dreadful word,
  The sails their swelling bosom spread
No longer must she stay aboard;
  They kiss'd, she sigh'd, he hung his head.
Her lessening boat unwilling rows to land;
'Adieu!' she cries; and waved her lily hand.

JOHN GAY (1685–1732)
Poems

INNOCENTS AT HOME

———— ·ɛɛɛ✿ɔɔɔ· ————

David Copperfield has married his child-wife Dora and taken on her dog Jip as a third-party risk.

Everybody we had anything to do with seemed to cheat us. Our appearance in a shop was a signal for the damaged goods to be brought out immediately. If we bought a lobster, it was full of water. All our meat turned out to be tough, and there was hardly any crust to our loaves. In search of the principle on which joints ought to be roasted, to be roasted enough, and not too much, I myself referred to the Cookery Book, and found it there established as the allowance of a quarter of an hour to every pound, and say a quarter over. But the principle always failed us by some curious fatality, and we never could hit any medium between redness and cinders.

I had reason to believe that in accomplishing these failures we incurred a far greater expense than if we had achieved a series of triumphs. It appeared to me, on looking over the tradesmen's books, as if we might have kept the basement story paved with butter, such was the extensive scale of our consumption of that article. I don't know whether the Excise returns of the period may have exhibited any increase in the demand for pepper; but if our performances did not affect the market, I should say several families must have left off using it. And the most wonderful fact of all was, that we never had anything in the house.

As to the washerwoman pawning the clothes, and coming in a state of penitent intoxication to apologise, I suppose that might have happened several times to anybody. Also the chimney on fire, the parish engine, and perjury on the part of the Beadle. But I apprehend that we were personally unfortunate in engaging a servant with a taste for cordials, who swelled our running account for porter at the public-house by such inexplicable items as 'quartern rum shrub (Mrs. C.);'

'Half-quartern gin and cloves (Mrs. C.);' 'Glass rum and peppermint (Mrs. C.)'—the parentheses always referring to Dora, who was supposed, it appeared on explanation, to have imbibed the whole of these refreshments.

One of our first feats in the housekeeping way was a little dinner to Traddles. I met him in town, and asked him to walk out with me that afternoon. He readily consenting, I wrote to Dora, saying I would bring him home. It was pleasant weather, and on the road we made my domestic happiness the theme of conversation. Traddles was very full of it; and said, that, picturing himself with such a home, and Sophy waiting and preparing for him, he could think of nothing wanting to complete his bliss.

I could not have wished for a prettier little wife at the opposite end of the table, but I certainly could have wished, when we sat down, for a little more room. I did not know how it was, but though there were only two of us, we were at once always cramped for room, and yet had always room enough to lose anything in. I suspect it may have been because nothing had a place of its own, except Jip's pagoda, which invariably blocked up the main thoroughfare. On the present occasion, Traddles was so hemmed in by the pagoda and the guitar-case, and Dora's flower-painting, and my writing-table, that I had serious doubts of the possibility of his using his knife and fork; but he protested, with his own good-humour, 'Oceans of room, Copperfield! I assure you, Oceans!'

There was another thing I could have wished; namely, that Jip had never been encouraged to walk about the table-cloth during dinner. I began to think there was something disorderly in his being there at all, even if he had not been in the habit of putting his foot in the salt or the melted-butter. On this occasion he seemed to think he was introduced expressly to keep Traddles at bay; and he barked at my old friend, and made short runs at his plate, with such undaunted pertinacity, that he may be said to have engrossed the conversation.

However, as I knew how tender-hearted my dear Dora was,

and how sensitive she would be to any slight upon her favourite, I hinted no objection. For similar reasons I made no allusion to the skirmishing plates upon the floor; or to the disreputable appearance of the castors, which were all at sixes and sevens, and looked drunk; or to the further blockade of Traddles by wandering vegetable dishes and jugs. I could not help wondering in my own mind, as I contemplated the boiled leg of mutton before me, previous to carving it, how it came to pass that our joints of meat were of such extraordinary shapes—and whether our butcher contracted for all the deformed sheep that came into the world; but I kept my reflections to myself.

'My love,' said I to Dora, 'what have you got in that dish?'

I could not imagine why Dora had been making tempting little faces at me, as if she wanted to kiss me.

'Oysters, dear,' said Dora, timidly.

'Was that *your* thought?' said I, delighted.

'Ye-yes, Doady,' said Dora.

'There never was a happier one!' I exclaimed, laying down the carving-knife and fork. 'There is nothing Traddles likes so much!'

'Ye-yes, Doady,' said Dora, 'and so I bought a beautiful little barrel of them, and the man said they were very good. But I—I am afraid there's something the matter with them. They don't seem right.' Here Dora shook her head, and diamonds twinkled in her eyes.

'They are only opened in both shells,' said I. 'Take the top one off, my love.'

'But it won't come off,' said Dora, trying very hard, and looking very much distressed.

'Do you know, Copperfield,' said Traddles, cheerfully examining the dish, 'I think it is in consequence—they are capital oysters, but I *think* it is in consequence—of their never having been opened.'

They never had been opened; and we had no oyster-knives—and couldn't have used them if we had; so we looked at the oysters and ate the mutton. At least we ate as much of it as was done, and made up with capers. If I had permitted him, I am satisfied that Traddles would have made a perfect savage of himself, and eaten a plateful of raw meat, to express enjoyment of the repast; but I would hear of no such immolation on the altar of friendship; and we had a course of bacon instead; there happening, by good fortune, to be cold bacon in the larder.

CHARLES DICKENS (1812–1870)
David Copperfield, Chap. 44

MAY AND DECEMBER

What can a young lassie, what shall a young lassie,
    What can a young lassie do wi' an auld man?
Bad luck on the pennie that tempted my minnie[1]
    To sell her poor Jenny for siller an' lan'!
       Bad Luck on the pennie, etc.

He's always compleenin' frae mornin' to e'enin',
    He hosts[2] and he hirples[3] the weary day lang;
He's doyl't[4] and he's dozin',[5] his bluid it is frozen,—
    O, dreary's the night wi' a crazy auld man!
       He's doyl't and he's dozin', etc.

He hums and he hankers, he frets and he cankers;
    I never can please him, do a' that I can;
He's peevish and jealous of a' the young fellows:
    O, dool[6] on the day I met wi'an auld man!
       He's peevish and jealous, etc.

My auld auntie Katie upon me tak's pity,
    I'll do my endeavour to follow her plan!
I'll cross him, and wrack him, until I heartbreak him,
    And then his auld brass will buy me a new pan.
       I'll cross him, and wrack him, etc.

ROBERT BURNS (1759–1796)
Songs

[1] Mother.   [2] Coughs.   [3] Limps.
[4] Crazed.   [5] Benumbed.   [6] Woe.

THE DYING HUSBAND'S FAREWELL

My dearest consort, my more loved heart,
I leave thee now; with thee all earthly joying,
Heaven knows with thee alone I sadly part:
All other earthly sweets have had their cloying;
   Yet never full of thy sweet loves' enjoying,
   Thy constant loves, next Heaven, I did refer them:
Had not much grace prevail'd, 'fore Heav'n I should
     prefer them.

I leave them, now the trumpet calls away;
In vain thine eyes beg for some time's reprieving;
Yet in my children here immortal stay;
In one I die, in many ones am living:
   In them, and for them, stay thy too much grieving:
   Look but on them, in them thou still wilt see
Married with thee again thy twice-two Antony.

And when with little hands, they stroke thy face,
As in thy lap they sit (ah, careless!) playing,
And stammering ask a kiss, give them a brace;
The last from me: and then a little staying,
   And in their face some part of me surveying,
   In them give me a third, and with a tear
Show thy dear love to him, who loved thee ever dear.

And now our falling house leans all on thee;
This little nation to thy care commend them:
In thee it lies that hence they want not me;
Themselves yet cannot, then the more defend them:
   And when green age permits, to goodness bend them:
   A mother were you once, now both you are;
Then with this double style double your love and care.

*

Farewell, farewell! I feel my long, long rest,
And iron sleep, my leaden heart oppressing:
Night after day, sleep after labour's best;
Port after storms, joy after long distressing;
   So weep thy loss, as knowing 'tis my blessing:
    Both as widow and a Christian grieve:
Still live I in thy thoughts, but as in Heaven I live.

Phineas Fletcher (1582–1650)
Poems

TRANSATLANTIC HEAVEN

With the sound of King George's trumpets, all the vain hopes of the weak and foolish young Pretender were blown away; and with that music, too, I may say, the drama of my own life was ended. That happiness, which hath subsequently crowned it, cannot be written in words; 'tis of its nature sacred and secret, and not to be spoken of, though the heart be ever so full of thankfulness, save to Heaven and the One Ear alone—to one fond being, the truest, and tenderest, and purest wife ever man was blest with. As I think of the immense happiness which was in store for me, and of the depth and intensity of that love which, for so many years, hath blessed me, I own to a transport of wonder and gratitude for such a boon—nay, am thankful to have been endowed with a heart capable of feeling and knowing the immense beauty and value of the gift which God hath bestowed upon me. Sure, love *vincit omnia*; is immeasurably above all ambition, more precious than wealth, more noble than name. He knows not life who knows not that; he hath not felt the highest faculty of the soul who hath not enjoyed it. In the name of my wife, I write the completion of hope and the summit of happiness. To have such a love is the one blessing, in comparison of which all earthly joy is of no value; and to think of her is to praise God.

It was at Bruxelles, whither we retreated after the failure of our plot—our Whig friends advising us to keep out of the way—that the great joy of my life was bestowed upon me, and that my dear mistress became my wife. We had been so accustomed to an extreme intimacy and confidence, and had lived so long and tenderly together, that we might have gone on to the end without thinking of a closer tie; but circumstances brought about that event which so prodigiously multiplied my happiness and hers (for which I humbly thank Heaven), although a calamity befell us, which, I blush to think, hath occurred more than once in our house.

I know not what infatuation of ambition urged the beautiful and wayward woman, whose name hath occupied so many of these pages, and who was served by me with ten years of such constant fidelity and passion, but ever after that day at Castlewood, when we rescued her, she persisted in holding all her family as her enemies, and left us, and escaped to France, to what a fate I disdain to tell. Nor was her son's house a home for my dear mistress; my poor Frank was weak, as perhaps all our race hath been, and led by women. Those around him were imperious, and in a terror of his mother's influence over him, lest he should recant, and deny the creed which he had adopted by their persuasion. The difference of their religion separated the son and the mother. My dearest mistress felt that she was severed from her children, and alone in the world—alone but for one constant servant, on whose fidelity, praised be Heaven! she could count. 'Twas after a scene of ignoble quarrel on the part of Frank's wife and mother (for the poor lad had been made to marry the whole of that German family with whom he had connected himself) that I found my mistress one day in tears, and then besought her to confide herself to the care and devotion of one who, by God's help, would never forsake her. And then the tender matron, as beautiful in her autumn, and as pure as virgins in their spring, with blushes of love and 'eyes of meek surrender', yielded to my respectful importunity, and consented to share my home. Let the last words I write thank her, and bless her who hath blessed it.

By the kindness of Mr. Addison, all danger of prosecution, and every obstacle against our return to England, was removed; and my son Frank's gallantry in Scotland made his peace with the King's government. But we two cared no longer to live in England; and Frank formally and joyfully yielded over to us the possession of that estate which we now occupy, far away from Europe and its troubles, on the beautiful banks of the Potomac, where we have built a new Castlewood, and think with grateful hearts of our old home. In our Transatlantic country we have a season, the calmest and most delightful of the year, which we call the Indian summer: I often say the autumn of our life resembles that happy and serene weather, and am thankful for its rest and its sweet sunshine. Heaven hath blessed us with a child, which each parent loves for her resemblance to the other. Our diamonds are turned into ploughs and axes for our plantations; and into negroes, the happiest and merriest, I think, in all this country: and the only jewel by which my wife sets any store, and from which she hath never parted, is that gold button she took from my arm on the day when she visited me in prison, and which she wore ever after, as she told me, on the tenderest heart in the world.

W. M. THACKERAY (1811–1863)
The History of Henry Esmond, Book III, Chap. 13

THE SAILOR'S WIFE

And are ye sure the news is true?
   And are ye sure he's weel?
Is this a time to think o' wark?
   Ye jades, lay by your wheel;
Is this the time to spin a thread,
   When Colin's at the door?
Reach down my cloak, I'll to the quay,
   And see him come ashore,
For there's nae luck about the house,
   There's nae luck at a';
There's little pleasure in the house
   When our gudeman's awa'.

And gie to me my bigonet,
   My bishop's satin gown;
For I maun tell the baillie's wife
   That Colin's in the town.
My Turkey slippers maun gae on,
   My stockins pearly blue;
It's a' to pleasure our gudeman,
   For he's baith leal and true.

Rise, lass, and mak a clean fireside,
   Put on the muckle pot;
Gie little Kate her button gown
   And Jock his Sunday coat;
And mak their shoon as black as slaes,
   Their hose as white as snaw;
It's a' to please my ain gudeman,
   For he's been long awa'.

There's twa fat hens upo' the coop
  Been fed this month and mair;
Mak haste and thraw their necks about,
  That Colin weel may fare;
And spread the table neat and clean,
  Gar ilka thing look braw,
For wha can tell how Colin fared
  When he was far awa'?

Sae true his heart, sae smooth his speech,
  His breath like caller air;
His very foot has music in't
  As he comes up the stair—
And will I see his face again?
  And will I hear him speak?
I'm downright dizzy wi' the thought,
  In troth I'm like to greet!

If Colin's weel, and weel content,
  I hae nae mair to crave:
And gin I live to keep him sae,
  I'm blest aboon the lave:
And will I see his face again,
  And will I hear him speak?
I'm downright dizzy wi' the thought,
  In troth I'm like to greet,
For there's nae luck about the house,
  There's nae luck at a';
There's little pleasure in the house
  When our gudeman's awa'.

W. J. MICKLE (1734–1788)
Songs

REUNION DENIED

Methought I saw my late espoused Saint
  Brought to me like *Alcestis* from the grave,
  Whom *Joves* great Son to her glad Husband gave,
  Rescu'd from death by force though pale and faint.
Mine as whom washt from spot of child-bed taint,
  Purification in the old Law did save,
  And such, as yet once more I trust to have
  Full sight of her in Heaven without restraint,
Came vested all in white, pure as her mind:
  Her face was vail'd, yet to my fancied sight,
  Love, sweetness, goodness, in her person shin'd
So clear, as in no face with more delight.
  But O as to embrace me she enclin'd
  I wak'd, she fled, and day brought back my night.

JOHN MILTON (1608–1674)
Sonnets

CAPTAIN OTTER AND HIS
BEAR-WHELP

Captain Otter, 'a Land and Sea Captain', is drinking with Dauphine and Clerimont.

Dauphine. Captain He-Otter, your She-Otter is coming, your wife.

Otter. Wife! buz? *titivilitium!* There's no such thing in nature. I confess, gentlemen, I have a cook, a laundress, a house-drudge, that serves my necessary turns, and goes under that title; but he's an ass that will be so uxorious to tie his affections to one circle. Come, the name dulls appetite. Here, replenish again; another bout. (*Fills the cups again.*) Wives are nasty, sluttish animals. A wife is a scurvy clogdogdo, an unlucky thing, a very foresaid bear-whelp, without any good fashion or breeding, *malabestia.*

Re-enter Truewit behind, with Mistress Otter.

Dauphine. Why did you marry one then, captain?

Otter. A pox!—I married with six thousand pound, I. I was in love with that. I have not kissed my Fury these forty weeks.

Clerimont. The more to blame you, captain.

Truewit. Nay, mistress Otter, hear him a little first.

Otter. She has a breath worse than my grandmother's.

Mrs. Otter. O treacherous liar! kiss me, sweet Master Truewit, and prove him a slandering knave.

Truewit. I'll rather believe you, lady.

Otter. And she has a peruke that's like a pound of hemp, made up in shoe-threads.

Mrs. Otter. O viper, mandrake!

Otter. O most vile face! and yet she spends me forty pound a year in mercury and hogs-bones. All her teeth were made in the Blackfriars, both her eyebrows in the Strand, and her hair in Silver Street. Every part of the town owns a piece of her.

Mrs. Otter (comes forward). I cannot hold.

Otter. She takes herself asunder still when she goes to bed, into some twenty boxes; and about next day noon is put together again, like a great German clock: and so comes forth, and rings a tedious 'larum to the whole house, and then is quiet again for an hour, but for her quarters—Have you done me right, gentlemen?

Mrs. Otter (falls upon him and beats him). No, sir, I'll do you right with my quarters, with my quarters.

Otter. O, hold, good princess.

Truewit. Sound, sound!   *Drum and trumpets sound.*

Clerimont. A battle, a battle!

Mrs. Otter. You notorious stinkardly bearward, does my breath smell?

Otter. Under correction, dear princess.—Look to my bear and my horse, gentlemen.

Mrs. Otter. Do I want teeth, and eyebrows, thou bull-dog?

Truewit. Sound, sound still.   *They sound again.*

Otter. No, I protest, under correction—

Mrs. Otter. Ay, now you are under correction, you protest: but you did not protest before correction, sir. Thou Judas, to offer to betray thy princess! I'll make thee an example.

Beats him.

BEN JONSON (1573–1637)
The Silent Woman, Act IV, Scene I

To students of vocabulary Ben Jonson's comedies are a perpetual feast. Titivilitium is Latin for a trifle; Anglicized as Titivel it was used of any light nave. Clogdogdo appears to be a compound suggestion of hindrance and cur or bitch. The allusion to Silver Street as a source of Mrs. Otter's peruke is interesting since it was there that Shakespeare lodged in the early years of the seventeenth century in the house of Christopher Mountjoy, a Huguenot maker of 'tires' or head-dresses and of wigs. The date of Ben Jonson's play is 1609.

N

FLINT AND ROSES

I couldn't touch a stop and turn a screw,
  And set the blooming world a-work for me,
Like such as cut their teeth—I hope, like you—
  On the handle of a skeleton gold key;
I cut mine on a leek, which I eat it every week:
  I'm a clerk at thirty bob as you can see.

But I don't allow it's luck and all a toss;
  There's no such thing as being starred and crossed;
It's just the power of some to be a boss,
  And the bally power of others to be bossed:
I face the music, sir; you bet I ain't a cur;
  Strike me lucky if I don't believe I'm lost!

For like a mole I journey in the dark,
  A-travelling along the underground
From my Pillar'd Halls and broad Suburbean Park,
  To come the daily dull official round;
And home again at night with my pipe all alight,
  A-scheming how to count ten bob a pound.

And it's often very cold and very wet,
  And my missis stitches towels for a hunks;
And the Pillar'd Halls is half of it to let—
  Three rooms about the size of travelling trunks.
And we cough, my wife and I, to dislocate a sigh,
  When the noisy little kids are in their bunks.

But you never hear her do a growl or whine,
  For she's made of flint and roses, very odd;
And I've got to cut my meaning rather fine,
  Or I'd blubber, for I'm made of greens and sod:
So p'r'aps we are in Hell for all that I can tell,
  And lost and damn'd and served up hot to God.

I ain't blaspheming, Mr. Silver-tongue;
  I'm saying things a bit beyond your art:
Of all the rummy starts you ever sprung,
  Thirty bob a week's the rummiest start!
With your science and your books and your the'ries about
                                            spooks,
  Did you ever hear of looking in your heart?

I didn't mean your pocket, Mr., no:
  I mean that having children and a wife,
With thirty bob on which to come and go,
  Isn't dancing to the tabor and the fife:
When it doesn't make you drink, by Heaven! it makes you
                                            think,
  And notice curious items about life.

JOHN DAVIDSON (1857–1909)
'Thirty Bob a Week', *Ballads and Songs*

SIR KENELM AND LADY VENETIA

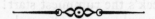

Sir Kenelm Digby, son of Sir Everard Digby who was executed for his share in the Gunpowder Plot was, in the view of John Aubrey, 'the most accomplished cavalier of his time'.

Much against his mother's, etc., consent, he married that celebrated beautie and courtezane, Mrs. Venetia Stanley.

Venetia Stanley was daughter of Sir Edward Stanley. She was a most beautifull desireable creature; and being *matura viro* was left by her father to live with a tenant and servants at Enston-abbey (his land, or the earl of Derby's) in Oxfordshire; but as private as that place was, it seemes her beautie could not lye hid. The young eagles had espied her, and she was sanguine and tractable, and of much suavity (which to abuse was greate pittie).

In those dayes Richard, earle of Dorset (eldest son and heire to the Lord Treasurer), lived in the greatest splendor of any nobleman of England. Among other pleasures that he enjoyed, Venus was not the least. This pretty creature's fame quickly came to his Lordship's eares, who made no delay to catch at such an opportunity.

I have now forgott who first brought her to towne, but I have heard my uncle Danvers say (who was her contemporary) that she was so commonly courted, and that by grandees, that 'twas written over her lodging one night *in literis uncialibus*,

Pray Come not Neer,
For Dame Venetia Stanley Lodgeth Here.

The earle of Dorset, aforesayd, was her greatest gallant, who was extremely enamoured of her, and had one if not more children by her. He setled on her an annuity of 500 *li. per annum.*

Among other young sparkes of that time, Sir Kenelme Digby grew acquainted with her, and fell so much in love with her that he married her, much against the good will of his mother; but he would say that 'a wise man, and lusty, could make an honest woman out of a brothell-house'. Sir Edmund Wyld had her picture (and you may imagine was very familiar with her), which picture is now at Droitwytch, in Worcestershire, at an inne, where now the towne keepe their meetings. Also at Mr. Rose's, a jeweller in Henrietta-street in Covent garden, is an excellent piece of hers, drawne after she was newly dead.

She had a most lovely and sweet-turn'd face, delicate darke-browne haire. She had a perfect healthy constitution; strong; good skin; well proportioned; much enclining to a *Bona Roba* (near altogether). Her face, a short ovall; darke-browne eie-browe about which much sweetness, as also in the opening of her eie-lids. The colour of her cheekes was just that of the damaske rose, which is neither too hott nor too pale. She was of a just stature, not very tall.

At Goathurst, in Bucks, is a rare originall picture of Sir Kenelme Digby and his lady Venetia, in one piece, by the hand of Sir Anthony van Dyke. In Ben. Johnson's 2d volume is a poeme called 'Eupheme, left to posteritie, of the noble lady, the ladie Venetia Digby, late wife of Sir Kenelme Digby, knight, a gentleman absolute in all numbers: consisting of these ten pieces, viz. Dedication of her Cradle; Song of her Descent; Picture of her Bodie; Picture of her Mind; Her being chose a Muse; Her faire Offices; Her happy Match; Her hopefull Issue; Her Apotheosis or Relation to the Saints; Her Inscription, or Crowne.' Sir Kenelme had severall pictures of her by Vandyke, etc. Her picture drawn by Sir Anthony Vandyke hangs in the queene's drawing-roome, at Windsor-castle, over the chimney. Her picture by Vandyke is now at Abermarleys, in Carmarthenshire, at Mr. Cornwalleys' sonne's widowe's (the lady Cornwalleys's) howse, who was the daughter and heire of Jones, of Abermarles. He had her hands cast in playster, and her feet, and her face. See Ben: Johnson's 2d volume, where he hath made her live in poetrey, in his drawing of her both body and mind:——

Sitting, and ready to be drawne,
What makes these tiffany, silkes, and lawne,
Embroideries, feathers, fringes, lace,
When every limbe takes like a face!—etc.

When these verses were made she had three children by
Sir Kenelme, who are there mentioned, viz. Kenelme, George,
and John.

She dyed in her bed suddenly. Some suspected that she was
poysoned. When her head was opened there was found but
little braine, which her husband imputed to her drinking of
viper-wine; but spitefull woemen would say 'twas a viper-
husband who was jealous of her that she would steale a leape.
I have heard some say that after her mariage she redeemed her
honour by her strick't living. Once a yeare the earle of Dorset
invited her and Sir Kenelme to dinner, where the earle would
behold her with much passion, and only kisse her hand.

JOHN AUBREY (1626–1697)
Brief Lives

SHAKESPEARIAN WIVES

(1) THE WARRIOR'S WIFE

Enter Lady Percy.

Hotspur. How now, Kate! I must leave you within these two
    hours.
Lady Percy. O, my good lord, why are you thus alone?
    For what offence have I this fortnight been
    A banisht woman from my Harry's bed?
    Tell me, sweet lord, what is't that takes from thee
    Thy stomach, pleasure, and thy golden sleep?
    Why dost thou bend thine eyes upon the earth,
    And start so often when thou sitt'st alone?
    Why hast thou lost the fresh blood in thy cheeks;
    And given my treasures and my rights of thee
    To thick-eyed musing and curst melancholy?
    In thy faint slumbers I by thee have watcht,
    And heard thee murmur tales of iron wars;
    Speak terms of manage to thy bounding steed;
    Cry, 'Courage! to the field!'—and thou hast talkt
    Of sallies and retires, of trenches, tents,
    Of palisadoes, frontiers, parapets,
    Of basilisks, of cannon, culverin,
    Of prisoners' ransom, and of soldiers slain,
    And all the currents of a heady fight.
    Thy spirit within thee hath been so at war,
    And thus hath so bestirr'd thee in thy sleep,
    That beads of sweat have stood upon thy brow,
    Like bubbles in a late-disturbed stream;
    And in thy face strange motions have appear'd,
    Such as we see when men restrain their breath
    On some great sudden hest. O, what portents are these?
    Some heavy business hath my lord in hand,
    And I must know it, else he loves me not.

Hotspur. What, ho!

Enter a Servant.

Hotspur. Is Gilliams with the packet gone?

Servant. He is, my lord, an hour ago.

Hotspur. Hath Butler brought those horses from the sheriff?

Servant. One horse, my lord, he brought even now.

Hotspur. What horse? a roan, a crop-ear, is it not?

Servant. It is, my lord.

Hotspur.   That roan shall be my throne.
    Well, I will back him straight: O esperance!—
    Bid Butler lead him forth into the park.

Exit Servant.

Lady Percy. But hear you, my lord.

Hotspur. What say'st thou, my lady?

Lady Percy. What is it carries you away?

Hotspur. Why, my horse,
    My love,—my horse.

Lady Percy.   Out, you mad-headed ape!
    A weasel hath not such a deal of spleen
    As you are tost with. In faith,
    I'll know your business, Harry,—that I will.
    I fear my brother Mortimer doth stir
    About his title, and hath sent for you
    To line his enterprise: but if you go,—

Hotspur. So far a-foot, I shall be weary, love.

Lady Percy. Come, come, you paraquito, answer me
    Directly unto this question that I ask:
    In faith, I'll break thy little finger, Harry,
    An if thou wilt not tell me all things true.

Hotspur. Away, away, you trifler!—Love?—I love thee not,
    I care not for thee, Kate: this is no world
    To play with mammets and to tilt with lips:
    We must have bloody noses and crackt crowns,
    And pass them current too.—God's me, my horse!—
    What say'st thou, Kate? what wouldst thou have with me?

Lady Percy. Do you not love me? do you not, indeed?
　　Well, do not, then; for since you love me not,
　　I will not love myself. Do you not love me?
　　Nay, tell me if you speak in jest or no.
Hotspur. Come, wilt thou see me ride?
　　And when I am o' horseback, I will swear
　　I love thee infinitely. But hark you, Kate;
　　I must not have you henceforth question me
　　Whither I go, nor reason whereabout:
　　Whither I must, I must; and, to conclude,
　　This evening must I leave you, gentle Kate.
　　I know you wise; but yet no further wise
　　Than Harry Percy's wife: constant you are;
　　But yet a woman: and for secrecy,
　　No lady closer; for I well believe
　　Thou wilt not utter what thou dost not know,—
　　And so far will I trust thee, gentle Kate.
Lady Percy. How! so far?
Hotspur. Not an inch further. But hark you, Kate:
　　Whither I go, thither shall you go too;
　　To-day will I set forth, to-morrow you.—
　　Will this content you, Kate?
Lady Percy. It must of force.

WILLIAM SHAKESPEARE (1564–1616)
King Henry the Fourth, Part I, Act II, Scene III

(2) THE OBEDIENT WIFE

Katharina. Fie, fie! unknit that threatening unkind brow:
　　And dart not scornful glances from those eyes,
　　To wound thy lord, thy king, thy governor:
　　It blots thy beauty, as frosts do bite the meads;
　　Confounds thy fame, as whirlwinds shake fair buds;

And in no sense is meet or amiable.
A woman moved is like a fountain troubled,
Muddy, ill-seeming, thick, bereft of beauty;
And while it is so, none so dry or thirsty
Will deign to sip, or touch one drop of it.
Thy husband is thy lord, thy life, thy keeper,
Thy head, thy sovereign; one that cares for thee,
And for thy maintenance commits his body
To painful labour both by sea and land,
To watch the night in storms, the day in cold,
Whilst thou liest warm at home, secure and safe;
And craves no other tribute at thy hands
But love, fair looks, and true obedience,—
Too little payment for so great a debt.
Such duty as the subject owes the prince,
Even such a woman oweth to her husband;
And when she is froward, peevish, sullen, sour,
And not obedient to his honest will,
What is she but a foul contending rebel,
And graceless traitor to her loving lord?
I am ashamed that women are so simple
To offer war, where they should kneel for peace;
Or seek for rule, supremacy, and sway,
When they are bound to serve, love, and obey.
Why are our bodies soft and weak and smooth,
Unapt to toil and trouble in the world?
But that our soft conditions and our hearts
Should well agree with our external parts?
Come, come, you froward and unable worms!
My mind hath been as big as one of yours,
My heart as great; my reason, haply, more,
To bandy word for word and frown for frown:
But now I see our lances are but straws;
Our strength as weak, our weakness past compare,—
That seeming to be most, which we indeed least are.
Then vail your stomachs, for it is no boot,
And place your hands below your husband's foot:

In token of which duty, if he please,
My hand is ready, may it do him ease.

WILLIAM SHAKESPEARE (1564–1616)
The Taming of the Shrew, Act V, Scene 2

This speech is now frequently delivered on the stage with a wink in the eye and a clear suggestion of tongue in the cheek. Was that Shakespeare's intention? Certainly the taste of our age would have it so. Kate's last words 'may it do him ease' can easily be spoken with an intimation of mockery and the last two lines of the play also indicate suspicion as to the genuineness of the surrender. Hortensio says as Petruchio goes out with Kate,

Now go thy ways, thou hast tamed a curst shrew.

To this Lucentio replies

Tis a wonder, by your leave, she will be tamed so.

So, on the mention of wonder as to the issue, we too may well be left in surmise.

(3) THE SHEPHERD'S WIFE

Shepherd. Fie, daughter! when my old wife lived, upon
This day she was both pantler, butler, cook;
Both dame and servant; welcomed all; served all;
Would sing her song and dance her turn; now here,
At upper end o' the table, now i' the middle;
On his shoulder, and his; her face o'fire
With labour, and the thing she took to quench it,
She would to each one sip. You are retired,
As if you were a feasted one, and not
The hostess of the meeting: pray you, bid
These unknown friends to's welcome; for it is
A way to make us better friends, more known.
Come, quench your blushes, and present yourself
That which you are, mistress o' the feast: come on,
And bid us welcome to your sheep-shearing,
As your good flock shall prosper.

WILLIAM SHAKESPEARE (1564–1616)
The Winter's Tale, Act IV, Scene 3

A NOT UNUSUAL CASE

It may be so: their love was never fire,
Never 'a wonder and a wild desire',
What brought them first together?
    What 'come hither'?
And what does that concern us now, or them?
Now, though life's whole vast various multitude
Were at their choice, and Venus wildly wooed
  With every stratagem,
    I still conclude
They would not alter much, nor dally far.
They, happiest in not following some queer star,
On usual roads, by frequent course, combined,
Are one, they mean one; them no tragic find,
Caprice, inversion, egotism shall break.
They are as children at the same good table,
Whom wisdom plenishes; whether bread or cake,
It is their common lot; not all are able
To count on daily sustenance; and this
Regular through long years is better bliss
Than chancing kickshaws. So, I guess, they live.
I wonder when it happened, their last kiss;
But maybe more than any kiss can give
Dwells in their composition: smile who will,
They thread the maze that baffles beauty still.

EDMUND BLUNDEN (1896-   )
Collected Poems

WIFE TO A ROYALIST

Sir John Penruddock, whose family had suffered severe losses by fighting for King Charles in the Civil War, led an abortive resurrection against Cromwell in March 1655. Capturing Salisbury and proclaiming Charles II as King, he marched west to gather support in Devon and Cornwall but was taken at South Molton, tried for High Treason at Exeter, and convicted and executed there in May of that year. His wife wrote this last letter to him.

My dear Heart,

My sad parting was so far from making me forget you, that I scarce thought upon myself since, but wholly upon you. Those dear embraces which I yet feel, and shall never lose, being the faithful testimonies of an indulgent husband, have charmed my soul to such a reverence of your remembrance, that were it possible, I would, with my own blood, cement your dead limbs to live again, and (with reverence) think it no sin to rob Heaven a little longer of a martyr. Oh! my dear, you must now pardon my passion, this being my last (oh, fatal word!) that ever you will receive from me; and know, that until the last minute that I can imagine you shall live, I shall sacrifice the prayers of a Christian, and the groans of an afflicted wife. And when you are not (which sure by sympathy I shall know), I shall wish my own dissolution with you, so that we may go hand in hand to Heaven. 'Tis too late to tell you what I have, or rather have not done for you; how being turned out of doors because I came to beg mercy; the Lord lay not your blood to their charge.

I would fain discourse longer with you, but dare not; passion begins to drown my reason, and will rob me of my devoirs, which is all I have left to serve you. Adieu, therefore, ten thousand times, my dearest dear; and since I must never see you more, take this prayer—May your faith be so strengthened that your constancy may continue; and then I know

Heaven will receive you; whither grief and love will in a short time (I hope) translate,

My dear,

Your sad, but constant wife, even to love your ashes when dead,

Arundel Penruddock

May the 3rd, 1655, eleven o'clock at night. Your children beg your blessing, and present their duties to you.

SISTERLY CONDUCT

'It's narrow, narrow, mak your bed,
　And learn to lie your lane;
For I'm gaun owre the sea, Fair Annie,
　A braw bride to bring hame.
Wi' her I will get gowd and gear,
　Wi' you I ne'er gat nane.

'But wha will bake my bridal bread,
　Or brew my bridal ale?
And wha will welcome my bright bride,
　That I bring owre the dale?'—

'It's I will bake your bridal bread,
　And brew your bridal ale;
And I will welcome your bright bride,
　That you bring owre the dale.'—

'But she that welcomes my bright bride
　Maun gang like maiden fair;
She maun lace on her robe sae jimp,[1]
　And comely braid her hair.

'Bind up, bind up your yellow hair,
　And tie it on your neck;
And see you look as maiden-like
　As the day that first we met.'—

'O how can I gang maiden-like,
　When maiden I am nane?
Have I not borne six sons to thee,
　And am wi' child again?'—

[1] Slender, trim.

'I'll put cooks into my kitchen,
  And stewards in my hall,
And I'll have bakers for my bread,
  And brewers for my ale;
But you're welcome to my bright bride,
  That I bring owre the dale.'

Three months and a day were gane and past,
  Fair Annie she gat word
That her love's ship was come at last,
  Wi' his bright young bride aboard.

She's ta'en her young son in her arms,
  Anither in her hand;
And she's gane up to the highest tower,
  Looks over sea and land.

'Come doun, come doun, my mother dear,
  Come aff the castle wa'!
I fear if langer ye stand there,
  Ye'll let yoursell doun fa'.'

She's ta'en a cake o' the best bread,
  A stoup o' the best wine,
And a' the keys upon her arm,
  And to the yett¹ is gane.

'O ye're welcome hame, my ain gude lord,
  To your castles and your towers;
Ye're welcome hame, my ain gude lord,
  To your ha's, but and your bowers.
And welcome to your hame, fair lady!
  For a' that's here is yours.'

'O whatna lady's that, my lord,
  That welcomes you and me?
Gin I be lang about this place,
  Her friend I mean to be.'

¹ Gate.

Fair Annie served the lang tables
    Wi' the white bread and the wine;
But ay she drank the wan water
    To keep her colour fine.

And aye she served the lang tables
    Wi' the white bread and the brown,
And aye she turn'd her round about,
    Sae fast the tears fell doun.

She took a napkin lang and white,
    And hung it on a pin;
It was to wipe away the tears,
    As she gaed out and in.

When bells were rung and mass was sung,
    And a' men bound for bed,
The bridegroom and the bonny bride
    In ae chamber were laid.

Fair Annie's ta'en a harp in her hand,
    To harp thir twa asleep;
But ay, as she harpit and she sang,
    Fu' sairly did she weep.

*

Then out and spak the bonny young bride,
    In bride-bed where she lay:
'That's like my sister Annie,' she says;
    'Wha is it doth sing and play?

'I'll put on my gown,' said the new-come bride,
    'And my shoes upon my feet;
I will see wha doth sae sadly sing,
    And what is it gars her greet.

o

'What ails you, what ails you, my housekeeper,
    That ye mak sic a mane?
Has ony wine-barrel cast its girds,
    Or is a' your white bread gane?'—

'It isna because my wine is spilt,
    Or that my white bread's gane;
But because I've lost my true love's love,
    And he's wed to anither ane.'—

'Noo tell me wha was your father,' she says,
    'Noo tell me wha was your mither?
And had ye ony sister?' she says,
    'And had ye ever a brither?'—

'The Earl of Wemyss was my father,
    The Countess of Wemyss my mither,
Young Elinor was my sister dear,
    And Lord John he was my brither.'—

'If the Earl of Wemyss was your father,
    I wot sae was he mine;
And it's O my sister Annie!
    Your love ye sallna tyne.'[1]

'Tak your husband, my sister dear;
    You ne'er were wrang'd for me,
Beyond a kiss o' his merry mouth
    As we cam owre the sea.

'Seven ships, loaded weel,
    Cam owre the sea wi' me;
Ane o' them, will tak me hame,
    And six I'll gie to thee.'

ANON (date uncertain)
Scottish Ballad of *Fair Annie*

[1] Lose.

TEAZLE TROUBLES

━━━━━━◄━◦◦◦◦◦◦◦◦═►━━━━━━

The School for Scandal was not a rapidly written successor to *The Rivals*. It was based on two earlier but abandoned pieces, one called *The Teazles* and the other *The Slanderers*. The second was better known to Sheridan's friends as *The Sneerwell Play*. In the former Sir Peter was presented as a re-marrying widower and in *The School for Scandal* as an old bachelor who is 'committing wedlock'. The two drafts were re-written and united with brilliant results. It is interesting to see how Sir Peter's first monologue was cut and made more effective for the actor speaking the lines. Therefore both passages are given.

Old Teazle (alone). In the year 44, I married my first wife; the wedding was at the end of the year—aye, 'twas in December; yet, before Ann. Dom. 45, I repented. A month before, we swore we preferred each other to the whole world—perhaps we spoke truth; but, when we came to promise to love each other till death, there I am sure we lied. Well, Fortune owed me a good turn; in 48 she died. Ah, silly Solomon, in 52 I find thee married again! Here, too, is a catalogue of ills—Thomas, born February 12; Jane, born Jan. 6; so they go on to the number of five. However, by death I stand credited but by one. Well, Margery, rest her soul! was a queer creature; when she was gone, I felt awkward at first, and being sensible that wishes availed nothing, I often wished for her return. For ten years more I kept my senses and lived single. Oh, blockhead, dolt Solomon! Within this twelve-month thou art married again—married to a woman thirty years younger than thyself; a fashionable woman. Yet I took her with caution; she had been educated in the country; but now she has more extravagance than the daughter of an Earl, more levity than a Countess. What a defect it is in our laws, that man who has once been branded in the forehead should be hanged for the second offence.

The Teazles, Act 1, Scene 1

Enter Sir Peter.

Sir Peter Teazle. When an old bachelor marries a young wife, what is he to expect? 'Tis now six months since Lady Teazle made me the happiest of men—and I have been the most miserable dog ever since that ever committed wedlock! We tift a little going to church, and came to a quarrel before the bells had done ringing. I was more than once nearly choked with gall during the honeymoon, and had lost all comfort in life before my friends had done wishing me joy. Yet I chose with caution—a girl bred wholly in the country, who never knew luxury beyond one silk gown, nor dissipation beyond the annual gala of a race ball. Yet now she plays her part in all the extravagant fopperies of the fashion and the town, with as ready a grace as if she had never seen a bush or a grass-plot out of Grosvenor Square! I am sneered at by all my acquaintance, and paragraphed in the newspapers. She dissipates my fortune, and contradicts all my humours; yet, the worst of it is, I doubt I love her, or I should never bear all this. However, I'll never be weak enough to own it.

R. B. SHERIDAN (1751–1816)
The School for Scandal, Act 1, Scene 2

THE BROWNINGS

THE WAYS OF LOVE

If thou must love me, let it be for nought
Except for love's sake only. Do not say
"I love her for her smile—her look—her way
Of speaking gently,—for a trick of thought
That falls in well with mine, and certes brought
A sense of pleasant ease on such a day"—
For these things in themselves, Beloved, may
Be changed, or change for thee,—and love, so wrought,
May be unwrought so. Neither love me for
Thine own dear pity's wiping my cheeks dry,—
A creature might forget to weep, who bore
The comfort long, and lose thy love thereby!
But love me for love's sake, that evermore
Thou mayst love on, through love's eternity.

*

How do I love thee? Let me count the ways.
I love thee to the depth and breadth and height
My soul can reach, when feeling out of sight
For the ends of Being and ideal Grace.
I love thee to the level of everyday's
Most quiet need, by sun and candle-light.
I love thee freely, as men strive for Right;
I love thee purely, as they turn from Praise.
I love thee with the passion put to use
In my old griefs, and with my childhood's faith
I love thee with a love I seemed to lose
With my lost saints,—I love thee with the breath,
Smiles, tears, of all my life!—and, if God choose,
I shall but love thee better after death.

ELIZABETH BARRETT BROWNING (1806–1861)
Sonnets from the Portuguese

THE MOON OF LOVE

What were seen? None knows, none ever shall know.
Only this is sure—the sight were other,
Not the moon's same side, born late in Florence,
Dying now impoverished here in London.
God be thanked, the meanest of his creatures
Boasts two soul-sides, one to face the world with,
One to show a woman when he loves her!

This I say of me, but think of you, Love!
This to you—yourself my moon of poets!
Ah, but that's the world's side, there's the wonder,
Thus they see you, praise you, think they know you
There, in turn I stand with them and praise you—
Out of my own self, I dare to phrase it.
But the best is when I glide from out them,
Cross a step or two of dubious twilight,
Come out on the other side, the novel
Silent silver lights and darks undreamed of,
Where I hush and bless myself with silence.
Oh, their Rafael of the dear Madonnas,
Oh, their Dante of the dread Inferno,
Wrote one song—and in my brain I sing it,
Drew one angel!—borne, see, on my bosom!

From *One Word More*

RE-UNION

Fear death?—to feel the fog in my throat,
　The mist in my face,
When the snows begin, and the blasts denote
　I am nearing the place,
The power of the night, the press of the storm,
　The post of the foe;
Where he stands, the Arch Fear in a visible form,
　Yet the strong man must go:

For the journey is done and the summit attain'd,
   And the barriers fall,
Though a battle's to fight ere the guerdon be gain'd,
   The reward of it all.
I was ever a fighter, so—one fight more,
   The best and the last!
I would hate that death bandaged my eyes, and forbore,
   And bade me creep past.
No! let me taste the whole of it, fare like my peers
   The heroes of old,
Bear the brunt, in a minute pay glad life's arrears
   Of pain, darkness and cold.
For sudden the worst turns the best to the brave,
   The black minute's at end,
And the element's rage, the fiend-voices that rave,
   Shall dwindle, shall blend,
Shall change, shall become first a peace out of pain,
   Then a light, then thy breast,
O thou soul of my soul! I shall clasp thee again,
   And with God be the rest!

ROBERT BROWNING (1812–1889)
Prospice

A FAITHFUL FRIEND

How near me came the hand of Death,
　When at my side he struck my dear,
And took away the precious breath
　Which quicken'd my beloved peer!
　　How helpless am I thereby made!
　　By day how grieved, by night how sad!
And now my life's delight is gone,
　—Alas! how am I left alone!

The voice which I did more esteem
　Than music in her sweetest key,
Those eyes which unto me did seem
　More comfortable than the day;
　　Those now by me, as they have been,
　　Shall never more be heard or seen;
But what I once enjoy'd in them
Shall seem hereafter as a dream.

Lord! keep me faithful to the trust
　Which my dear spouse reposed in me:
To him now dead preserve me just
　In all that should performed be!
　　For though our being man and wife
　　Extendeth only to this life,
Yet neither life nor death should end
The being of a faithful friend.

GEORGE WITHER (1588–1667)
A Widow's Hymn

CANDIDA

Candida, wife of the Rev. James Mavor Morell, genial and popular East End Socialist parson but 'pardonably vain of his powers and unconsciously pleased with himself', has entertained in their home the seemingly weak and helpless poet, Eugene Marchbanks. When he makes love to her she has to point out that it is her husband who needs protection. All his life, women have made him what he is, his wife not least.

Candida (smiling a little). Let us sit and talk comfortably over it like three friends. (*To Morell*) Sit down, dear. (*Morell takes the chair from the fireside—the children's chair.*) Bring me that chair, Eugene. (*She indicates the easy chair. He fetches it silently, even with something like cold strength, and places it next Morell, a little behind him. She sits down. He goes to the sofa and sits there, still silent and inscrutable. When they are all settled she begins, throwing a spell of quietness on them by her calm, sane, tender tone.*) You remember what you told me about yourself, Eugene: how nobody has cared for you since your old nurse died: how those clever, fashionable sisters and successful brothers of yours were your mother's and father's pets: how miserable you were at Eton: how your father is trying to starve you into returning to Oxford: how you have had to live without comfort or welcome or refuge, always lonely, and nearly always disliked and misunderstood, poor boy!

Marchbanks (faithful to the nobility of his lot). I had my books. I had Nature. And at last I met you.

Candida. Never mind that just at present. Now I want you to look at this other boy here—my boy—spoiled from his cradle. We go once a fortnight to see his parents. You should come with us, Eugene, and see the pictures of the hero of that household. James as a baby! the most wonderful of all babies. James holding his first school prize, won at the ripe age of eight! James as the captain of his eleven! James in his first frock coat! James under all sorts of glorious circumstances!

You know how strong he is (I hope he didn't hurt you)—
how clever he is—how happy! (*With deepening gravity*) Ask
James's mother and his three sisters and wife and mother to
his children all in one. Ask Prossy and Maria how troublesome
the house is even when we have no visitors to help us to slice
the onions. Ask the tradesmen who want to worry James and
spoil his beautiful sermons who it is that puts them off. When
there is money to give, he gives it: when there is money to
refuse, I refuse it. I build a castle of comfort and indulgence
and love for him, and stand sentinel always to keep little
vulgar cares out. I make him master here, though he does not
know it, and could not tell you a moment ago how it came to
be so. (*With sweet irony*) And when he thought I might go
away with you, his only anxiety was—what should become
of me! And to tempt me to stay he offered me (*leaning forward
to stroke his hair caressingly at each phrase*) his strength for my
defence, his industry for my livelihood, his position for my
dignity, his—(*relenting*) ah, I am mixing up your beautiful
sentences and spoiling them, am I not, darling? (*She lays her
cheek fondly against his.*)

   Morell (*quite overcome, kneeling beside her chair and embracing
her with boyish ingenuousness*). It's all true, every word. What
I am you made me with the labor of your hands and the love
of your heart. You are my wife, my mother, my sisters; you
are the sum of all loving care to me.

   Candida (*in his arms, smiling, to Eugene*). Am I your mother
and sisters to you, Eugene?

   Marchbanks (*rising with a fierce gesture of disgust*). Ah, never.
Out, then, into the night with me!

G. BERNARD SHAW (1856–1950)
Candida, Act III

TROUBLE ABOUT A CLOAK

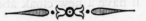

This winter's weather it waxeth cold,
 And frost it freezeth on every hill,
And Boreas blows his blast so bold
 That all our cattle are like to spill.
Bell, my wife, she loves no strife;
 She said unto me quietlye,
'Rise up, and save cow Crumbock's life.
 Man, put thine old cloak about thee!'

He. 'O Bell, my wife, why dost thou flyte?[1]
 Thou kens my cloak is very thin:
It is so bare and over worn,
 And cricke thereon cannot renn.
Then I'll no longer borrow nor lend;
 For once I'll new apparell'd be;
To-morrow I'll to town and spend;
 For I'll have a new cloak about me.'

She. 'Cow Crumbock is a very good cow;
 She had been always true to the pail;
She has helped us to butter and cheese, I trow,
 And other things she will not fail.
I would be loth to see her pine.
 Good husband, counsel take of me:
It is not for us to go so fine—
 Man, take thine old cloak about thee!'

He. 'My cloak it was a very good cloak,
 It hath been always true to the wear;
But now it is not worth a groat:
 I have had it four and forty year,

[1] Scold.

Sometime it was of cloth in grain:[1]
    'Tis now but a sigh clout,[2] as you may see:
It will neither hold out wind nor rain;
    And I'll have a new cloak about me.'

She. 'It is four and forty years ago
    Since the one of us the other did ken;
And we have had, betwixt us two,
    Of children either nine or ten.
We have brought them up to women and men:
    In the fear of God I trow they be.
And why wilt thou thyself misken?
    Man, take thine old cloak about thee!'

He. 'O Bell, my wife, why dost thou flyte?
    Now is now, and then was then:
Seek now all the world throughout,
    Thou kens not clowns from gentlemen:
They are clad in black, green, yellow and blue,
    So far above their own degree.
Once in my life I'll take a view;
    For I'll have a new cloak about me.'

She. 'King Stephen was a worthy peer;
    His breeches cost him but a crown;
He held them sixpence all too dear,
    Therefore he called the tailor 'lown'.[3]
He was a king and wore the crown,
    And thou'se but of a low degree:
It's pride that puts this country down:
    Man, take thy old cloak about thee!'

[1] Scarlet cloth.
[3] A rag for straining.
[3] Loon, rogue. Shakespeare quotes this quatrain with slight alterations as a song for Iago in *Othello*, Act 2, Scene 3.

He. Bell, my wife, she loves not strife,
　　Yet she will lead me, if she can;
And to maintain an easy life
　　I oft must yield, though I'm good-man.
It's not for a man with a woman to threap,[1]
　　Unless he first give o'er the plea:
As we began, so we will keep,
　　And I'll take my old cloak about me.

ANON. (medieval)

[1] Contend.

EPITAPH

To these, whom Death again did wed,
This grave's their second marriage-bed;
For though the hand of Fate could force
'Twixt soul and body a divorce,
It could not sunder man and wife
Because they both lived but one life.
Peace, good Reader, do not weep,
Peace, the lovers are asleep.
They, sweet turtles, folded lie
In the last knot that Love could tie.
And though they lie as they were dead,
Their pillow stone, their sheets of lead,
Pillow hard, and sheets not warm,
Love made the bed: they'll take no harm;
Let them sleep: let them sleep on,
Till this stormy night be gone,
And the eternal morrow dawn;
Then the curtains will be drawn,
And they wake into a light,
Whose day shall never die in night.

RICHARD CRASHAW (1612–1649)
Poems

PART FOUR

OPINION AND ADVICE

COURTSHIP—A CAUTION

Never love unless you can
Bear with all the faults of man!
Men sometimes will jealous be
Though but little cause they see,
And hang the head as discontent,
And speak what straight they will repent.

Men, that but one Saint adore,
Make a show of love to more;
Beauty must be scorn'd in none,
Though but truly served in one:
For what is courtship but disguise?
True hearts may have dissembling eyes.

Men, when their affairs require,
Must awhile themselves retire;
Sometimes hunt, and sometimes hawk,
And not ever sit and talk:—
If these and such-like you can bear,
Then like, and love, and never fear!

THOMAS CAMPION (1567–1620)
Poems

P

DISPOSING OF DAUGHTERS

It is a truth universally acknowledged, that a single man in possession of a good fortune must be in want of a wife.

However little known the feelings or views of such a man may be on his first entering a neighbourhood, this truth is so well fixed in the minds of the surrounding families, that he is considered as the rightful property of some one or other of their daughters.

'My dear Mr. Bennet,' said his lady to him one day, 'have you heard that Netherfield Park is let at last?'

Mr. Bennet replied that he had not.

'But it is,' returned she; 'for Mrs. Long has just been here, and she told me all about it.'

Mr. Bennet made no answer.

'Do not you want to know who has taken it?' cried his wife impatiently.

'*You* want to tell me, and I have no objection to hearing it.'

This was invitation enough.

'Why, my dear, you must know, Mrs. Long says that Netherfield is taken by a young man of large fortune from the north of England; that he came down on Monday in a chaise and four to see the place, and was so much delighted with it, that he agreed with Mr. Morris immediately; that he is to take possession before Michaelmas, and some of his servants are to be in the house by the end of next week.'

'What is his name?'

'Bingley.'

'Is he married or single?'

'Oh! single, my dear, to be sure! A single man of large fortune; four or five thousand a-year. What a fine thing for our girls!'

'How so? how can it affect them?'

'My dear Mr. Bennet,' replied his wife, 'how can you be so tiresome, you must know that I am thinking of his marrying one of them.'

'Is that his design in settling here?'

'Design! nonsense, how can you talk so! But it is very likely that he *may* fall in love with one of them, and therefore you must visit him as soon as he comes.'

'I see no occasion for that. You and the girls may go, or you may send them by themselves, which perhaps will be still better, for as you are as handsome as any of them, Mr. Bingley might like you the best of the party.'

'My dear, you flatter me. I certainly *have* had my share of beauty, but I do not pretend to be anything extraordinary now. When a woman has five grown-up daughters, she ought to give over thinking of her own beauty.'

'In such cases, a woman has not often much beauty to think of.'

'But, my dear, you must indeed go and see Mr. Bingley when he comes into the neighbourhood.'

'It is more than I engage for, I assure you.'

'But consider your daughters. Only think what an establishment it would be for one of them. Sir William and Lady Lucas are determined to go, merely on that account, for in general, you know, they visit no new-comers. Indeed you must go, for it will be impossible for *us* to visit him if you do not.'

'You are over-scrupulous, surely. I dare say Mr. Bingley will be very glad to see you; and I will send a few lines by you to assure him of my hearty consent to his marrying whichever he chuses of the girls: though I must throw in a good word for my little Lizzy.'

'I desire you will do no such thing. Lizzy is not a bit better than the others; and I am sure she is not half so handsome as Jane, nor half so good-humoured as Lydia. But you are always giving *her* the preference.'

'They have none of them much to recommend them,' replied he; 'they are all silly and ignorant, like other girls; but Lizzy has something more of quickness than her sisters.'

'Mr. Bennet, how can you abuse your own children in such a way! You take delight in vexing me. You have no compassion on my poor nerves.'

'You mistake me, my dear. I have a high respect for your nerves. They are my old friends. I have heard you mention them with consideration these twenty years at least.'

'Ah! you do not know what I suffer.'

'But I hope you will get over it, and live to see many young men of four thousand a-year come into the neighbourhood.'

'It will be no use to us, if twenty such should come, since you will not visit them.'

'Depend upon it, my dear, that when there are twenty, I will visit them all.'

Mr. Bennet was so odd a mixture of quick parts, sarcastic humour, reserve, and caprice, that the experience of three-and-twenty years had been insufficient to make his wife understand his character. *Her* mind was less difficult to develope. She was a woman of mean understanding, little information, and uncertain temper. When she was discontented, she fancied herself nervous. The business of her life was to get her daughters married; its solace was visiting and news.

JANE AUSTEN (1775–1818)
Pride and Prejudice, Chap. I

SHAKESPEARIAN BREVITIES

—————•cec✪ɔɔɔ•—————

Men are April when they woo, December when they wed;
maids are May when they are maids, but the sky changes
when they are wives.

> Rosalind in *As You Like It*, Act IV, Scene 1

I may chance have some odd quirks and remnants of wit broken
on me, because I have rail'd so long against marriage. But
doth not the appetite alter? A man loves the meat in his youth
that he cannot endure in his age. Shall quips and sentences
and these paper-bullets of the brain awe a man from the career
of his humour? No, the world must be peopled. When I said
I would die a bachelor, I did not think I would live till I were
married. Here comes Beatrice. By this day, she's a fair lady:
I do spy some marks of love in her.

> Benedick in *Much Ado About Nothing*, Act II, Scene III

Thou art an elm my husband—I a vine.
Whose weakness married to thy stronger state
Makes me with thy strength to communicate.
If aught possess thee from me, it is dross
Usurping ivy, brier, or idle moss.

> Adriana in *The Comedy of Errors*, Act II, Scene 2

Let still the woman take
An elder than herself: so wears she to him,
So sways she level in her husband's heart;
For, boy, however we do praise ourselves,
Our fancies are more giddy and unfirm
More longing, wavering, sooner lost and won
Than women's are.

> Duke Orsino in *Twelfth Night*, Act II, Scene IV

Imogen. Why did you throw your wedded lady from you?
    Think that you are upon a lock; and now
    Throw me again.   *Embracing Posthumus.*
Posthumus.   Hang there like fruit, my soul.
    Till the tree doth die.

                    Cymbeline, Act V, Scene V

WILLIAM SHAKESPEARE (1564—1616)

MONOGAMY AND MYSTICISM

The present fashions in love are not so definite and universal as those in clothes. It is as though our age were dubiously hesitating between crinolines and hobble skirts, trunk hose and Oxford trousers. Two distinct and hostile conceptions of love coexist in the minds of men and women, two sets of ideals, of conventions, of public opinions, struggle for the right to mould the psychological and physiological material of love. One is the conception evolved by the nineteenth century out of the ideals of Christianity on the one hand and romanticism on the other. The other is that still rather inchoate and negative conception which contemporary youth is in process of forming out of the materials provided by modern psychology.

The public opinion, the conventions, ideals, and prejudices which gave active force to the first convention and enabled it, to some extent at least, to modify the actual practice of love, had already lost much in their strength when they were rudely shattered, at any rate in the minds of the young, by the shock of the War. As usually happens, practice preceded theory, and the new conception of love was called in to justify existing post-War manners. Having gained a footing, the new conception is now a cause of new behaviour among the youngest adolescent generation, instead of being, as it was for the generation of the War, an explanation of war-time behaviour made after the fact.

Let us try to analyse these two coexisting and conflicting conceptions of love. The older conception was, as I have said, the product of Christianity and romanticism—a curious mixture of contradictions, of the ascetic dread of passion and the romantic worship of passion. Its ideal was a strict monogamy, such as St. Paul grudgingly conceded to amorous humanity, sanctified and made eternal by one of those terrific exclusive passions which are the favourite theme of poetry and drama. It is an ideal which finds its most characteristic expression in the poetry of that infinitely respectable rebel, that profoundly anglican worshipper of passion, Robert Browning. It was Rousseau who first started the cult of passion for passion's sake. Before his time the great passions, such as that of Paris for Helen, of Dido for Aeneas, of Paolo and Francesca for one another had been regarded rather as disastrous maladies than as enviable states of soul. Rousseau, followed by all the romantic poets of France and England, transformed the grand passion from what it had been in the Middle Ages—a demoniac possession—into a divine ecstasy, and promoted it from the rank of a disease to that of the only true and natural form of love. The nineteenth-century conception of love was thus doubly mystical, with the mysticism of Christian asceticism and sacramentalism, and with the romantic mysticism of Nature. It claimed an absolute rightness on the grounds of its divinity and of its naturalness.

Now, if there is one thing that the study of history and psychology makes abundantly clear, it is that there are no such things as either 'divine' or 'natural' forms of love. Innumerable gods have sanctioned and forbidden innumerable kinds of sexual behaviour, and innumerable philosophers and poets have advocated the return to the most diverse kinds of 'nature'. Every form of amorous behaviour, from chastity and monogamy to promiscuity and the most fantastic 'perversions', is found both among animals and men. In any given human society, at any given moment, love, as we have seen, is the result of the interaction of the unchanging instinctive and physiological material of sex with the local conventions of morality and religion, the local laws, prejudices, and ideals. The degree of permanence of these conventions, religious myths, and ideals is proportional to the social utility in the given circumstances of time and place.

ALDOUS HUXLEY (1894–   )
Do What You Will (1929)

SAMUEL BUTLER NOTES

Women sometimes say that they have had no offers, and only wish that some one had ever proposed to them. That is not the right way to put it. What they should say is that though, like all women, they have been proposing to men all their lives, yet they grieve to remember that they have been invariably refused.

The question of marriage or non-marriage is only the question of whether it is better to be spoiled one way or another.

In matrimony, to hesitate is sometimes to be saved.

Samuel Butler (1835–1902)
Note-Books, Section 7

LOOKING ON THE DARK SIDE

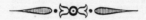

Even in the common affairs of life, in love, friendship, and
marriage, how little security have we when we trust our
happiness in the hands of others! Most of the friends I have
seen have turned out the bitterest enemies, or cold, uncomfortable acquaintance. Old companions are like meats served
up too often, that lose their relish and their wholesomeness.
He who looks at beauty to admire, to adore it, who reads of
its wondrous power in novels, in poems, or in plays, is not
unwise; but let no man fall in love, for from that moment he
is 'the baby of a girl'. I like very well to repeat such lines as
these in the play of 'Mirandola'

> 'With what a waving air she goes
> Along the corridor! How like a fawn!
> Yet statelier. Hark! No sound, however soft,
> Nor gentlest echo telleth when she treads,
> But every motion of her shape doth seem
> Hallowed by silence.'

But however beautiful the description, defend me from meeting
with the original!

> 'The fly that sips treacle
> Is lost in the sweets;
> So he that tastes woman
> Ruin meets.'

The song is Gay's, not mine, and a bitter-sweet it is.—How
few out of the infinite number of those that marry and are
given in marriage, wed with those they would prefer to all the
world; nay, how far the greater proportion are joined together
by mere motives of convenience, accident, recommendation of
friends, or indeed not infrequently by the very fear of the

event, by repugnance and a sort of fatal fascination: yet the
tie is for life, not to be shaken off but with disgrace or death:
a man no longer lives to himself, but is a body (as well as
mind) chained to another, in spite of himself.—

> 'Like life and death in disproportion met.'

So Milton (perhaps from his own experience) makes Adam
exclaim, in the vehemence of his despair,

>   'For either
> He never shall find out fit mate, but such
> As some misfortune brings him or mistake;
> Or whom he wishes most shall seldom gain
> Through her perverseness, but shall see her gain'd
> By far a worse; or if she love, withheld
> By parents; or his happiest choice too late
> Shall meet, already link'd and wedlock-bound
> To a fell adversary, his hate and shame;
> Which infinite calamity shall cause
> To human life, and household peace confound.'

If love at first sight were mutual, or to be conciliated by kind
offices; if the fondest affection were not so often repaid and
chilled by indifference and scorn; if so many lovers both
before and since the madman in Don Quixote had not "wor-
shipped a statue, hunted the wind, cried aloud to the desert";
if friendship were lasting; if merit were renown, and renown
were health, riches, and long life; or if the homage of the
world were paid to conscious worth and the true aspirations
after excellence, instead of its gaudy signs and outward
trappings; then indeed I might be of opinion that it is better
to live to others than one's-self; but as the case stands, I
incline to the negative side of the question.

William Hazlitt (1778–1830)
On Living to Oneself, *Table Talk*

A MERRY WIDOW, FREQUENTLY

Chaucer's Wife of Bath, that remarkable traveller who had been thrice to Jerusalem as well as five times to the altar, lost five husbands which, as Oscar Wilde's Lady Bracknell would have said, looks like carelessness. But the gaps were rapidly filled and in the Prologue to a tale told by one of the Canterbury Pilgrims the filling was vehemently justified. For ease of reading I have used Professor Coghill's translation whose claim to keep the spirit and rhythm of the orginal, while using a vocabulary which does not hinder fluent reading to-day, is well justified. The Wife was a racy character and one imagines the words pouring from her. To be slowed down by consulting a glossary is to be deprived of the Prologue's proper quality.

> If there were no authority on earth
> Except experience, mine, for what it's worth,
> And that's enough for me, all goes to show
> That marriage is a misery and a woe;
> For let me say, if I may make so bold,
> My lords, since when I was but twelve years old,
> Thanks be to God Eternal evermore,
> Five husbands have I had at the church door;
> Yes, it's a fact that I have had so many,
> All worthy in their way, as good as any.
>   'Someone said recently for my persuasion
> That as Christ only went on one occasion
> To grace a wedding—in Cana of Galilee—
> He taught me by example there to see
> That it is wrong to marry more than once.
> Consider, too, how sharply, for the nonce,
> He spoke, rebuking the Samaritan
> Beside the well, Christ Jesus, God and man.
> "Thou hast had five men husband unto thee
> And he that even now thou hast," said He,
> "Is not thy husband," Such the words that fell;
> But what He meant thereby I cannot tell.
> Why was her fifth—explain it if you can—

No lawful spouse to the Samaritan?
How many might have had her, then, to wife?
I've never heard any answer all my life
To give the number final definition.
People may guess or frame a supposition,
But I can say for certain it's no lie,
God bade us all to wax and multiply.
That kindly text I well can understand.
Is not my husband under God's command
To leave his father and mother and take me?
No word of what the number was to be,
Then why not marry two or even eight?
And why speak evil of the married state?

   'Take wise King Solomon of long ago;
We hear he had a thousand wives or so.
And would to God it were allowed to me
To be refreshed, aye, half so much as he!
He must have had a gift of God for wives,
No one to match him in a world of lives!
This noble king, one may as well admit,
On the first night threw many a merry fit
With each of them, he was so much alive.
Blessed be God that I have wedded five!
Welcome the sixth, whenever he appears.
I can't keep continent for years and years.
No sooner than one husband's dead and gone
Some other christian man shall take me on,
For then, so says the Apostle, I am free
To wed, o' God's name, where it pleases me.
Wedding's no sin, so far as I can learn.
Better it is to marry than to burn.

   'What do I care if people choose to see
Scandal in Lamech for his bigamy?
I know that Abraham was a holy man,
And Jacob too, for all that I can scan,
Yet each of them, we know, had several brides,
Like many another holy man besides.

Show me a time or text where God disparages
Or sets a prohibition upon marriages
Expressly, let me have it! Show it me!
And where did He command virginity?
I know as well as you do, never doubt it,
All the Apostle Paul had said about it;
He said that as for precepts he had none.
One may advise a woman to be one;
Advice is no commandment in my view.
He left it in our judgement what to do.
    'Had God commanded maidenhood to all
Marriage would be condemned beyond recall,
For clearly, if the seed were never sown,
How ever could virginity be grown?
Paul did not dare pronounce, let matters rest,
His Master having given him no behest.
There's a prize offered for virginity;
Catch as catch can! Who's in for it? Let's see!
    'It is not everyone who hears the call;
On whom God wills He lets His power fall.
The Apostle was a virgin, well I know;
Nevertheless though all his writings show
He wished that everyone were such as he,
It's all mere counsel to virginity.
And as for being married, he lets me do it
Out of indulgence, so there's nothing to it
In marrying me, suppose my husband dead;
There's nothing bigamous in such a bed.
Though it were good a man should never touch
A woman (meaning here in bed and such)
And dangerous to assemble fire and tow
—What this allusion means you all must know—
He only says virginity is fresh,
More perfect than the frailty of the flesh
In married life—except when he and she
Prefer to live in married chastity.
    'I grant it you. I'll never say a word

Decrying maidenhood although preferred
To frequent marriage; there are those who mean
To live in their virginity, as clean
In body as in soul, and never mate.
I'll make no boast about my own estate.
As in a noble household, we are told,
Not every dish and vessel's made of gold,
Some are of wood, yet earn their master's praise,
God calls His folk to Him in many ways.
To each of them God gave His proper gift,
Some this, some that, and left them to make shift.
   'Virginity is perfect, unforsaken,
Continence too, devoutly undertaken.
But Christ who of perfection is the well
Bade not that everyone should go and sell
All that he had and give it to the poor
To follow in His footsteps, that is sure.
He spoke to those that would live perfectly,
And by your leave, my lords, that's not for me.
I will bestow the flower of life, the honey,
Upon the acts and fruit of matrimony.'

GEOFFREY CHAUCER (1340?–1400)
The Canterbury Tales
The Wife of Bath's Prologue

HOLMES, WOMEN, AND DR. WATSON

Dr. Watson is talking to Sherlock Holmes.

'May I ask whether you have any professional inquiry on foot at present?'

'None. Hence the cocaine. I cannot live without brain-work. What else is there to live for? Stand at the window here. Was ever such a dreary, dismal, unprofitable world? See how the yellow fog swirls down the street and drifts across the dun-coloured houses. What could be more hopelessly prosaic and material? What is the use of having powers, doctor, when one has no field upon which to exert them? Crime is common-place, existence is commonplace, and no qualities save those which are commonplace have any function upon earth.'

With a crisp knock, our landlady entered, bearing a card upon the brass salver.

'A young lady for you, sir,' she said, addressing my companion.

'Miss Mary Morstan,' he read. 'Hum! I have no recollection of the name. Ask the young lady to step up, Mrs. Hudson. Don't go, doctor. I should prefer that you remain.'

Miss Morstan entered the room with a firm step and an outward composure of manner. She was a blonde young lady, small, dainty, well gloved, and dressed in the most perfect taste. There was, however, a plainness and simplicity about her costume which bore with it a suggestion of limited means. The dress was a sombre greyish beige, untrimmed and un-braided, and she wore a small turban of the same dull hue, relieved only by a suspicion of white feather in the side. Her face had neither regularity of feature nor beauty of complexion, but her expression was sweet and amiable, and her large blue eyes were singularly spiritual and sympathetic. In an experience of women which extends over many nations and three separate continents, I have never looked upon a face which gave a clearer promise of a refined and sensitive nature. I could not but observe that, as she took the seat which Sherlock Holmes placed for her, her lip trembled, her hand quivered, and she showed every sign of intense inward agitation.

'I have come to you, Mr. Holmes,' she said, 'because you once enabled my employer, Mrs. Cecil Forrester, to unravel a little domestic complication. She was much impressed by your kindness and skill.'

'Mrs. Cecil Forrester,' he repeated, thoughtfully. 'I believe that I was of some slight service to her. The case, however, as I remember it, was a very simple one.'

'She did not think so. But at least you cannot say the same of mine. I can hardly imagine anything more strange, more utterly inexplicable, than the situation in which I find myself.'

Holmes rubbed his hands, and his eyes glistened. He leaned forward in his chair with an expression of extraordinary concentration upon his clear-cut, hawk-like features.

'State your case,' said he, in brisk, business tones.

I felt that my position was an embarrassing one.

'You will, I am sure, excuse me,' I said, rising from my chair.

To my surprise, the young lady held up her gloved hand to detain me.

'If your friend,' she said, 'would be good enough to stop, he might be of inestimable service to me.'

I relapsed into my chair.

*

'Au revoir,' said our visitor; and with a bright, kindly glance from one to the other of us, she replaced her pearl-box in her bosom and hurried away.

Standing at the window, I watched her walking briskly down the street, until the grey turban and white feather were but a speck in the sombre crowd.

'What a very attractive woman!' I exclaimed, turning to my companion.

Q

He had lit his pipe again, and was leaning back with droop-ing eyelids. 'Is she?' he said, languidly; 'I did not observe.'

'You really are an automaton—a calculating machine,' I cried. 'There is something positively inhuman in you at times.'

He smiled gently.

'It is of the first importance,' he said, 'not to allow your judgment to be biased by personal qualities. A client is to me a mere unit, a factor in a problem. The emotional qualities are antagonistic to clear reasoning. I assure you that the most winning woman I ever knew was hanged for poisoning three little children for their insurance-money, and the most repel-lent man of my acquaintance is a philanthropist who has spent nearly a quarter of a million upon the London poor.'

'In this case, however—'

'I never make exceptions. An exception disproves the rule. Have you ever had occasion to study character in handwriting? What do you make of this fellow's scribble?'

'It is legible and regular,' I answered. 'A man of business habits and some force of character.'

Holmes shook his head.

'Look at his long letters,' he said. 'They hardly rise above the common herd. That d might be an a, and l an e. Men of character always differentiate their long letters, however illegibly they may write. There is vacillation in his k's and self-esteem in his capitals. I am going out now. I have some few references to make. Let me recommend this book—one of the most remarkable ever penned. It is Winwood Reade's Martyrdom of Man. I shall be back in an hour.'

I sat in the window with the volume in my hand, but my thoughts were far from the daring speculations of the writer. My mind ran upon our last visitor—her smiles, the deep, rich tones of her voice, the strange mystery which overhung her life. If she were seventeen at the time of her father's disappearance she must be seven-and-twenty now—a sweet age, when youth has lost its self-consciousness and become a little sobered by experience. So I sat and mused, until such dangerous thoughts came into my head that I hurried away to my desk and plunged furiously into the latest treatise upon pathology. What was I, an Army surgeon with a weak leg and a weaker banking account, that I should dare to think of such things? She was a unit, a factor—nothing more. If my future were black, it was better surely to face it like a man than to attempt to brighten it by mere will-o'-the wisps of the imagination.

*

The problem brought to Baker Street by Miss Morstan has been solved. Dr. Watson is discussing it and his next move.

'Well, and there is the end of our little drama,' I remarked, after we had sat some time smoking in silence. 'I fear that it may be the last investigation in which I shall have the chance of studying your methods. Miss Morstan has done me the honour to accept me as a husband in prospective.'

He gave a most dismal groan.

'I feared as much,' he said. 'I really cannot congratulate you.'

I was a little hurt.

'Have you any reason to be dissatisfied with my choice?' I asked.

'Not at all. I think she is one of the most charming young ladies I ever met, and might have been most useful in such work as we have been doing. She had a decided genius that way; witness the way in which she preserved the Agra plan from all the other papers of her father. But love is an emotional thing, and whatever is emotional is opposed to that true, cold reason which I place above all things. I should never marry myself, lest I bias my judgment.'

'I trust,' said I, laughing, 'that my judgment may survive the ordeal. But you look weary.'

'Yes, the reaction is already upon me. I shall be as limp as a rag for a week.'

'Strange,' said I, 'how terms of what in another man I should call laziness alternate with your fits of splendid energy and vigour.'

'Yes,' he answered, 'there are in me the makings of a very fine loafer, and also of a pretty spry sort of a fellow.'

'The division seems rather unfair,' I remarked. 'You have done all the work in this business. I get a wife out of it, Jones gets the credit; pray what remains for you?'

'For me,' said Sherlock Holmes, 'there still remains the cocaine-bottle.' And he stretched his long, white hand up for it.

Sir A. Conan Doyle (1859–1930)
The Sign of Four

No doubt it was a happy union. But Mrs. Watson must have had many lonely and anxious days and nights with her husband so often an absentee while he shared the perilous and exhausting triumphs of his anti-feminist hero.

MATCH-MAKING LADIES

When Adeline, in all her growing sense
   Of Juan's merits and his situation,
Felt on the whole an interest intense,—
   Partly perhaps because a fresh sensation,
Or that he had an air of innocence,
   Which is for innocence a sad temptation—
As women hate half measures, on the whole,
She 'gan to ponder how to save his soul.

She had a good opinion of advice,
   Like all who give and eke receive it gratis,
For which small thanks are still the market price,
   Even where the article at highest rate is:
She thought upon the subject twice or thrice,
   And morally decided, the best state is
For morals, marriage; and this question carried,
She seriously advised him to get married.

Juan replied, with all becoming deference,
   He had a predilection for that tie;
But that, at present, with immediate reference
   To his own circumstances, there might lie
Some difficulties, as in his own preference,
   Or that of her to whom he might apply:
That still he'd wed with such or such a lady,
If that they were not married all already.

Next to the making matches for herself,
   And daughters, brothers, sisters, kith or kin,
Arranging them like books on the same shelf,
   There's nothing women love to dabble in

More (like a stock-holder in growing pelf)
    Than match-making in general: 'tis no sin
Certes, but a preventative, and therefore
That is, no doubt, the only reason wherefore.

But never yet (except of course a miss
    Unwed, or mistress never to be wed,
Or wed already, who object to this)
    Was there chaste dame who had not in her head
Some drama of the marriage unities,
    Observed as strictly both at board and bed
As those of Aristotle, though sometimes
They turn out melodrames or pantomimes.

They generally have some only son
    Some heir to a large property, some friend
Of an old family, some gay Sir John,
    Or grave Lord George, with whom perhaps might end
A line, and leave posterity undone,
    Unless a marriage was applied to mend
The prospect and their morals: and besides,
They have at hand a blooming glut of brides.

From these they will be careful to select,
    For this an heiress, and for that a beauty;
For one a songstress who hath no defect,
    For 't other one who promises much duty;
For this a lady no one can reject,
    Whose sole accomplishments were quite a booty;
A second for her excellent connexions;
A third, because there can be no objections.

LORD BYRON (1788–1824)
Don Juan, Canto XV

DEAN SWIFT'S ADVICE

————— ·ccc✿ɔɔ· —————

Madam,

The hurry and impertinence of receiving and paying Visits on account of your Marriage, being now over, you are beginning to enter into a Course of Life, where you will want much Advice to divert you from falling into many Errors, Fopperies, and Follies to which your Sex is subject.

*

I must therefore desire you in the first place to be very slow in changing the modest behaviour of a virgin: It is usual in young wives before they have been many Weeks married, to assume a bold, forward Look and manner of Talking; as if they intended to signify in all Companies, that they were no longer Girls, and consequently that their whole Demeanor, before they got a Husband, was all but a Countenance and Constraint upon their Nature: Whereas, I suppose, if the Votes of wise Men were gathered, a very great Majority would be in favour of those Ladies, who after they were entered into that State, rather chose to double their portion of Modesty and Reservedness.

I must likewise warn you strictly against the least degree of Fondness to your Husband before any Witness whatsoever, even before your nearest Relations, or the very Maids of your Chamber. This proceeding is so exceeding odious and disgustful to all who have either good Breeding or good Sense, that they assign two very unamiable Reasons for it; the one is gross Hypocrisy, and the other has too bad a Name to mention. If there is any difference to be made, your Husband is the lowest Person in Company, either at Home or Abroad, and every Gentleman present has a better Claim to all marks of Civility and Distinction from you. Conceal your Esteem and Love in your own Breast, and reserve your kind Looks and Language for Private hours, which are so many in the Four and Twenty, that they will afford time to employ a Passion as exalted as any that was ever described in a *French* Romance.

Upon this Head, I should likewise advise you to differ in Practice from those Ladies who affect abundance of Uneasiness while their Husbands are abroad, start with every Knock at the Door, and ring the Bell incessantly for the Servants to let in their Master; will not eat a bit at Dinner or Supper if the Husband happens to stay out, and receive him at his return with such a Medly of chiding and kindness, and catechising him where he has been, that a Shrew from Billingsgate would be a more easy and eligible Companion.

Of the same leaven are those Wives, who when their Husbands are gone a Journey, must have a Letter every Post, upon pain of Fits and Hystericks, and a day must be fixed for their return home without the least allowance for Business, or Sickness, or Accidents, or Weather: Upon which, I can only say that in my observation, those Ladies who were apt to make the greatest clutter upon such occasions, would liberally have paid a Messenger for bringing them news that their Husbands had broken their Necks on the Road.

You will perhaps be offended when I advise you to abate a little of that violent Passion for fine Cloaths, so predominant in your Sex. It is a little hard, that ours, for whose sake you wear them, are not admitted to be of your Council: I may venture to assure you that we will make an abatement at any time of Four Pounds a yard in a Brocade, if the Ladies will allow a suitable addition of care in the Cleanliness and Sweetness of their Persons: For, the satyrical part of mankind will needs believe, that it is not impossible, to be very fine and very filthy; and that the Capacities of a Lady are sometimes apt to fall short in cultivating Cleanliness and Finery together. I shall only add, upon so tender a subject, what a pleasant Gentleman said concerning a silly Woman of quality; that nothing could make her supportable but cutting off her head, for his Ears were offended by her Tongue, and his Nose by her Hair and Teeth.

*

I advise that your company at home should consist of Men, rather than Woman. To say the truth, I never yet knew a tolerable Woman to be fond of her own Sex: I confess, when both are mixt and well chosen, and put their best qualities forward, there may be an intercourse of civility and good-will; which, with the addition of some degree of sense, can make conversation or any amusement agreeable. But a Knot of Ladies, got together by themselves, is a very school of Impertinence and Detraction, and it is well if those be the worst.

Let your Men-acquaintance be of your Husband's choice, and not recommended to you by any She-companions; because they will certainly fix a Coxcomb upon you, and it will cost you some time and pains before you can arrive at the knowledge of distinguishing such a one from a Man of Sense.

*

There is never wanting in this Town, a tribe of bold, swaggering, rattling Ladies, whose Talents pass among Coxcombs for Wit and Humour; their excellency lies in rude choquing Expression, and what they call *running a Man down*. If a Gentleman in their Company happens to have any Blemish in his Birth or Person, if any misfortune hath befallen his Family or himself, for which he is ashamed, they will be sure to give him broad Hints of it without any Provocation. I would recommend you to the acquaintance of a common Prostitute, rather than to that of such Termagants as these. I have often thought that no Man is obliged to suppose such Creatures to be Women; but to treat them like insolent Rascals disguised in Female Habits, who ought to be stripp'd and kick'd down stairs.

I will add one thing although it be a little out of place, which is to desire that you will learn to value and exteem your Husband for those good Qualities which he really possesseth, and not to fancy others in him which he certainly hath not. For although this latter is generally understood to be a mark of Love, yet it is indeed nothing but Affectation and ill Judgment.

It is true, he wants so very few Accomplishments, that you are in no great danger of erring on this side: But my Caution is occasion'd by a Lady of your Acquaintance, married to a very valuable Person, whom yet she is so unfortunate as to be always commending for those Perfections to which he can least pretend.

I can give you no Advice upon the Article of Expence, only I think you ought to be well informed how much your Husband's Revenue amounts to, and be so good a Computer as to keep within it, in that part of the Management which falls to your share; and not to put youself in the number of those Politick Ladies, who think they gain a great Point when they have teazed their Husbands to buy them a new Equipage, a lac'd Head, or a fine Petticoat, without once considering what long Scores remain unpaid to the Butcher.

I desire you will keep this Letter in your Cabinet, and often examine impartially your whole Conduct by it: And so God bless you, and make you a fair Example to your Sex, and a perpetual Comfort to your Husband and your Parents.

I am, with great Truth and Affection,

Madam,

Your most faithful Friend
and humble Servant.

DEAN SWIFT (1667–1745)
Miscellanies of Prose & Verse,
Vol. 2—A Letter To a Very Young Lady

THE MAN-TRAP

Don Juan. In that case, what is virtue but the Trade Union-ism of the married? Let us face the facts, dear Ana. The Life Force respects marriage only because marriage is a contrivance of its own to secure the greatest number of children and the closest care of them. For honor, chastity, and all the rest of your moral figments it cares not a rap. Marriage is the most licentious of human institutions.—

Ana. Juan!

The Statue (protesting). Really!—

Don Juan (determinedly). I say the most licentious of human institutions: that is the secret of its popularity. And a woman seeking a husband is the most unscrupulous of all the beasts of prey. The confusion of marriage with morality has done more to destroy the conscience of the human race than any other single error. Come, Ana! do not look shocked: you know better than any of us that marriage is a man-trap baited with simulated accomplishments and delusive idealizations. When your sainted mother, by dint of scoldings and punishments, forced you to learn how to play half a dozen pieces on the spinet—which she hated as much as you did—had she any other purpose than to delude your suitors into the belief that your husband would have in his home an angel who would fill it with melody, or at least play him to sleep after dinner? You married my friend Ottavio: well, did you ever open the spinet from the hour when the Church united him to you?

Ana. You are a fool, Juan. A young married woman has something else to do than sit at the spinet without any support for her back; so she gets out of the habit of playing.

Don Juan. Not if she loves music. No: believe me, she only throws away the bait when the bird is in the net.

Ana (bitterly). And men, I suppose, never throw off the mask when their bird is in the net. The husband never becomes negligent, selfish, brutal—oh never!

Don Juan. What do these recriminations prove, Ana? Only that the hero is as gross an imposture as the heroine.

Ana. It is all nonsense: most marriages are perfectly comfortable.

Don Juan. 'Perfectly' is a strong expression, Ana. What you mean is that sensible people make the best of one another. Send me to the galleys and chain me to the felon whose number happens to be next before mine: and I must make the best of the companionship. Many such companionships, they tell me, are touchingly affectionate; and most are at least tolerably friendly. But that does not make a chain a desirable ornament nor the galleys an abode of bliss. Those who talk most about the blessings of marriage and the constancy of its vows are the very people who declare that if the chain were broken and the prisoners left free to choose, the whole social fabric would fly asunder. You cannot have the argument both ways. If the prisoner is happy, why lock him in? If he is not, why pretend that he is?

G. Bernard Shaw (1856–1950)
Man and Superman, Act III

A BACHELOR'S COMPLAINT

As a single man, I have spent a good deal of my time in noting down the infirmities of Married People, to console myself for those superior pleasures, which they tell me I have lost by remaining as I am.

I cannot say that the quarrels of men and their wives ever made any great impression upon me, or had much tendency to strengthen in those anti-social resolutions, which I took up long ago upon more substantial considerations. What oftenest offends me at the houses of married persons where I visit, is an error of quite a different description; it is that they are too loving.

Not too loving neither: that does not explain my meaning. Besides, why should that offend me? The very act of separating themselves from the rest of the world, to have the fuller enjoyment of each other's society, implies that they prefer one another to all the world.

But what I complain of is, that they carry this preference so undisguisedly, they perk it up in the faces of us single people so shamelessly, you cannot be in their company a moment without being made to feel, by some indirect hint or open avowal, that *you* are not the object of this preference. Now there are some things which give no offence, while implied or taken for granted merely; but expressed, there is much offence in them.

If a man were to accost the first homely-featured or plain-dressed young woman of his acquaintance, and tell her bluntly, that she was not handsome or rich enough for him, and he could not marry her, he would deserve to be kicked for his ill manners; yet no less is implied in the fact, that having access and opportunity of putting the question to her, he has never yet thought fit to do it. The young woman understands this as clearly as if it were put into words; but no reasonable young woman would think of making this the ground of a quarrel. Just as little right have a married couple to tell me by speeches, and looks that are scarce less plain than speeches, that I am not the happy man—the lady's choice. It is enough that I know I am not; I do not want this perpetual reminding.

The display of superior knowledge or riches may be made sufficiently mortifying; but these admit of a palliative. The knowledge which is brought out to insult me, may accidentally improve me; and in the rich man's houses and pictures—his parks and gardens, I have a temporary usufruct at least. But the display of married happiness has none of these palliatives: it is throughout pure, unrecompensed, unqualified insult.

Marriage by its best title is a monopoly, and not of the least invidious sort. It is the cunning of most possessors of any exclusive privilege to keep their advantage as much out of sight as possible, that their less favoured neighbours, seeing little of the benefit, may the less be disposed to question the right, but these married monopolists thrust the most obnoxious part of their patent into our faces.

Nothing is to me more distasteful than that entire complacency and satisfaction which beam in the countenances of a new-married couple—in that of the lady particularly: it tells you, that her lot is disposed of in this world: that *you* can have no hopes of her. It is true, I have none: nor wishes either, perhaps: but this is one of those truths which ought, as I said before, to be taken for granted, not expressed.

The excessive airs which those people give themselves, founded on the ignorance of us unmarried people, would be more offensive if they were less irrational. We will allow them to understand the mysteries belonging to their own craft better than we, who have not had the happiness to be made free of the company: but their arrogance is not content within these limits. If a single person presume to offer his opinion in their presence, though upon the most indifferent subject, he is immediately silenced as an incompetent person. Nay, a young married lady of my acquaintance, who, the best of the jest was, had not changed her condition above a fortnight before, in a question on which I had the misfortune to differ from her, respecting the properest mode of breeding oysters for the London market, had the assurance to ask with a sneer, how such an old Bachelor as I could pretend to know anything about such matters!

But what I have spoken of hitherto is nothing to the airs these creatures give themselves when they come, as they generally do, to have children. When I consider how little of a rarity children are—that every street and blind alley swarms with them—that the poorest people commonly have them in most abundance—that there are few marriages that are not blest with at least one of these bargains—how often they turn out ill, and defeat the fond hopes of their parents, taking to vicious courses, which end in poverty, disgrace, the gallows, etc.—I cannot for my life tell what cause for pride there can possibly be in having them. If they were young phoenixes, indeed, that were born but one in a year, there might be a pretext. But when they are so common . . .

I do not advert to the insolent merit which they assume with their husbands on these occasions. Let *them* look to that. But why *we*, who are not their natural-born subjects, should be expected to bring our spices, myrrh, and incense—our tribute and homage of admiration—I do not see.

"Like as the arrows in the hand of the giant, even so are the young children"; so says the excellent office in our Prayer-book appointed for the churching of women. "Happy is the man that hath his quiver full of them." So say I; but then don't let him discharge his quiver upon us that are weaponless; let them be arrows, but not to gall and stick us. I have generally observed that these arrows are double-headed: they have two forks, to be sure to hit with one or the other. As for instance, when you come into a house which is full of children, if you happen to take no notice of them (you are thinking of something else, perhaps, and turn a deaf ear to their innocent caresses), you are set down as untractable, morose, a hater of children. On the other hand, if you find them more than usually engaging—if you are taken with their pretty manners, and

set about in earnest to romp and play with them, some pretext
or other is sure to be found for sending them out of the room;
they are too noisy or boisterous, or Mr. —— does not like
children. With one or other of these folks the arrow is sure to
hit you.

I could forgive their jealousy, and dispense with toying
with their brats, if it gives them any pain; but I think it unreasonable to be called upon to *love* them, where I see no
occasion—to love a whole family, perhaps eight, nine, or ten,
indiscriminately—to love all the pretty dears, because children
are so engaging!

CHARLES LAMB (1775–1834)
A Bachelor's Complaint of the
Behaviour of Married People
Essays of Elia

SWEET-BREATH'D WOMAN

Give me the splendid silent sun with all his beams full-dazzling,
Give me juicy autumnal fruit ripe and red from the orchard,
Give me a field where the unmow'd grass grows,
Give me an arbour, give me the trellis'd grape,
Give me fresh corn and wheat, give me serene-moving animals
  teaching content,
Give me nights perfectly quiet as on high plateaus west of the
  Mississippi, and I looking up at the stars,
Give me odorous at sunrise a garden of beautiful flowers where
  I can walk undisturb'd,
Give me for marriage a sweet-breath'd woman of whom I
  should never tire,
Give me a perfect child, give me away aside from the noise of
  the world a rural domestic life,
Give me to warble spontaneous songs recluse by myself, for
  my own ears only,
Give me solitude, give me Nature, give me again, O Nature,
  your primal sanities!

WALT WHITMAN (1819–1892)

R

PANTAGRUEL PERPLEXED

(How Panurge asketh counsel of Pantagruel whether he should marry, yea, or nay)

Panurge prosecuted the discourse he had already broached, and therewithal fetching, as from the bottom of his heart, a very deep sigh, said, My lord and master, you have heard the design I am upon, which is to marry. I humbly beseech you, for the affection which of a long time you have borne me, to give me your best advice therein. Then, answered Pantagruel, seeing you have so decreed and taken deliberation thereon, and that the matter is fully determined, what need is there of any further talk thereof, but forthwith to put into execution what you have resolved? Yea, but, quoth Panurge, I would be loth to act anything therein without your counsel had thereto. It is my judgment also, quoth Pantagruel, and I advise you to it. Nevertheless, quoth Panurge, if I understood aright, that it were much better for me to remain a bachelor as I am, than to run headlong upon new hair-brained undertakings of conjugal adventure, I would rather choose not to marry. Quoth Pantagruel—Then do not marry. Yes, but quoth Panurge, would you have me so solitarily drag out the whole course of my life, without the comfort of a matrimonial consort? You know it is written: *Væ soli!* and a single person is never seen to reap the joy and solace that is found with married folks. Then marry, in the name of God, quoth Pantagruel.

But if, quoth Panurge, my wife should make me a cuckold; as it is not unknown unto you, how this hath been a very plentiful year in the production of that kind of cattle; I would fly off the hinges, and grow impatient beyond all measure and mean. I love cuckolds with all my heart, for they seem unto me to be of a right honest conversation, and I truly, do very willingly frequent their company; but should I die for it, I would not be one of their number. That is for me a too-sore prickling point. Then do not marry, quoth Pantagruel, for without all controversy this sentence of Seneca is infallibly true, What thou to others shalt have done, others will do the like to thee.

Do you, quoth Panurge, aver that without all exception? Yes, truly, quoth Pantagruel, without all exception. Ho, ho, says, Panurge, by the wrath of a little devil, his meaning is, either in this world, or in the other which is to come. Yet seeing I can no more do without a wife, than a blind man without his staff,—for the funnel must be in agitation, without which manner of occupation I cannot live,—were it not a great deal better for me to apply and associate myself to some one honest, lovely, and virtuous woman, than as I do, by a new change of females every day, run a hazard of being bastinadoed, or, (which is worse,) of the great pox, if not of both together. For never,—be it spoken, by their husbands' leave and favour, —had I enjoyment yet of an honest woman. Marry then, in God's name, quoth Pantagruel.

But if, quoth Panurge, it were the will of God, and that my destiny did unluckily lead me to marry an honest woman, who should beat me, I would be stored with more than two third parts of the patience of Job, if I were not stark mad by it, and quite distracted with such rugged dealings. For it hath been told me, that those exceeding honest women have ordinarily very wicked headpieces; therefore is it, that their family lacketh not for good vinegar. Yet in that case should it go worse with me, if I did not then in such sort bang her back and breast, so thumpingly bethwack her gillets, to wit, her arms, legs, head, lights, liver, and milt, with her other entrails, and mangle, jag, and slash her coats, so after the cross billet fashion, that the greatest devil of hell should wait at the gate for the reception of her damned soul. I could make a shift for this year to wave such molestation and disquiet, and be content to lay aside that trouble, and not to be engaged in it.

Do not marry then, answered Pantagruel. Yes, but, quoth Panurge, considering the condition wherein I now am, out of debt and unmarried; mark what I say, free from all debt, in an ill hour! for, were I deeply on the score, my creditors would be but too careful of my paternity, but being quit, and not married, nobody will be so regardful of me, or carry towards me a love like that which is said to be in a conjugal affection. And if by some mishap I should fall sick, I would be looked to very waywardly. The wise man saith, Where there is no women, I mean, the mother of a family, and wife in the union of a lawful wedlock, the crazy and diseased are in danger of being ill used, and of having much brabbling and strife about them: as by clear experience hath been made apparent in the persons of popes, legates, cardinals, bishops, abbots, priors, priests, and monks, But there, assure yourself, you shall not find me. Marry, then in the name of God, answered Pantagruel.

But if, quoth Panurge, being ill at ease, and possibly through that distemper made unable to discharge the matrimonial duty that is incumbent to an active husband, my wife, impatient of that drooping sickness, and faint-fits of a pining languishment, should abandon and prostitute herself to the embraces of another man, and not only then not help and assist me in my extremity and need, but withal flout at, and make sport of that my grievous distress and calamity; or peradventure, which is worse, embezzle my goods, and steal from me, as I have seen it oftentimes befall unto the lot of many other men, it were enough to undo me utterly, to fill brimful the cup of my misfortune, and make me play the mad-pate reeks of Bedlam. Do not marry then, quoth Pantagruel.

Yea, but, said Panurge, I shall never by any other means come to have lawful sons and daughters, in whom I may harbour some hope of perpetuating my name and arms, and to whom also I may leave and bequeath my inheritances and purchased goods, (of which latter sort you need not doubt, but that in some one or other of these mornings, I will make a fair and goodly show,) that so may I cheer up and make merry, when otherwise I should be plunged into a peevish sullen mood of pensive sullenness, as I do perceive daily by the gentle and loving carriage of your kind and gracious father towards you; as all honest folks use to do at their own homes, and private dwelling-houses. For being free from debt, and yet not married, if casually I should fret and be angry although the cause of my grief and displeasure were never so just, I am afraid, instead of consolation, that I should meet with nothing else but scoffs, frumps, gibes, and mocks at my disastrous fortune. Marry then, in the name of God, quoth Pantagruel; and thus have I given you my advice.

By François Rabelais
(about 1490–1553, exact dates uncertain)
The Heroic Deeds of Gargantua and Pantagruel
Translated (or transmuted) by Sir Thomas Urquhart
(1611–1660)

THE TOURIST'S MATRIMONIAL
GUIDE THROUGH SCOTLAND

Ye tourists, who Scotland would enter,
The summer and autumn to pass,
I'll tell you how far you may venture
To flirt with your lad or your lass;
How close you may come upon marriage,
Still keeping the wind of the law,
And not, by some foolish miscarriage,
Get woo'd and married an' a'.

Woo'd and married an' a',
Married and woo'd an' a';
And not by some foolish miscarriage
Get woo'd and married an' a'.

This maxim itself might content ye,
The marriage is made—by consent,
Provided it's done *de praesenti*,
And marriage is really what's meant.
Suppose that young Jocky or Jenny
Say "We two are husband and wife",
The witnesses needn't be many—
They're instantly buckled for life.

Woo'd and married an' a',
Married and woo'd an' a';
It isn't with us a hard thing
To get woo'd and married an' a'.

If people are drunk or delirious,
The marriage of course will be bad,
Or if they're not sober and serious,
But acting a play or charade.

It's bad if it's only a cover
    For cloaking a scandal or sin,
And talking a landlady over
    To let the folks lodge at her inn.

      Woo'd and married an' a',
      Married and woo'd an' a';
      It isn't the mere use of words
      Makes you woo'd and married an' a'.

You'd better keep clear of love-letters
    Or write them with caution and care;
For, faith they may fasten your fetters,
    If wearing a conjugal air.
Unless you're a knowing old stager,
    'Tis here you'll most likely be lost;
As a certain much-talked-about Major
    Had very near found to his cost.

      Woo'd and married an' a',
      Married and woo'd an' a';
      They are perilous things pen and ink,
      To get woo'd and married an' a'.

I ought to tell the unwary
    That into the noose they'll be led,
By giving a promise to marry,
    And acting as if they were wed.
But if, when the promise you're plighting,
    To keep it you think you'd be loath,
Just see that it isn't in writing,
    And then it must come to your oath.

      Woo'd and married an' a',
      Married and woo'd an' a';
      I've shown you a dodge to avoid
      Being woo'd and married an' a',

A third way of tying the tether,
  Which sometimes may happen to suit,
Is living a good while together,
  And getting a married repute,
But you who are here as a stranger,
  And don't mean to stay with us long,
Are little exposed to that danger;
  So here I may finish my song.

  Woo'd and married an' a',
  Married and woo'd an' a';
  You're taught now to seek or to shun
  Being woo'd and married an' a'.

LORD NEAVES (1800–1876)
Scottish Lord of Justiciary
Poems

TO WED OR NOT TO WED

He that hath wife and children hath given hostages to fortune; for they are impediments to great enterprises, either of virtue or mischief. Certainly, the best works, and of greatest merit for the public, have proceeded from the unmarried or childless men, which both in affection and means have married and endowed the public. Yet it were great reason that those that have children should have greatest care of future times; unto which they know they must transmit their dearest pledges. Some there are, who though they lead a single life, yet their thoughts do end with themselves, and account future times impertinences. Nay, there are some other that account wife and children but as bills of charges. Nay more, there are some foolish rich covetous men that take a pride in having no children, because they may be thought so much the richer. For perhaps they have heard some talk, *Such an one is a great rich man*, and another except to it, *Yea, but he hath a great charge of children*; as if it were an abatement to his riches.

But the most ordinary cause of a single life is liberty; especially in certain self-pleasing and humorous minds, which are so sensible of every restraint, as they will go near to think their girdles and garters to be bonds and shackles. Unmarried men are best friends, best masters, best servants; but not always best subjects; for they are light to run away; and almost all fugitives are of that condition. A single life doth well with churchmen; for charity will hardly water the ground where it must first fill a pool. It is indifferent for judges and magistrates; for if they be facile and corrupt, you shall have a servant five times worse than a wife. For soldiers, I find the generals commonly in their hortatives put men in mind of their wives and children; and I think the despising of marriage amongst the Turks maketh the vulgar soldier more base.

Certainly wife and children are a kind of discipline of

humanity; and single men, though they be many times more charitable, because their means are less exhaust, yet, on the other side, they are more cruel and hard-hearted (good to make severe inquisitors), because their tenderness is not so oft called upon. Grave natures, led by custom, and therefore constant, are commonly loving husbands; as was said of Ulysses, *Vetulam suam praetulit immortalitati.* Chaste women are often proud and forward, as presuming upon the merit of their chastity. It is one of the best bonds both of chastity and obedience in the wife, if she think her husband wise; which she will never do if she find him jealous.

Wives are young men's mistresses; companions for middle age; and old men's nurses. So as a man may have a quarrel to marry when he will. But yet he was reputed one of the wise men, that made answer to the question, when a man should marry *A young man not yet, an elder man not at all.* It is often seen that bad husbands have very good wives; whether it be that it raiseth the price of their husband's kindness when it comes; or that the wives take a pride in their patience. But this never fails, if the bad husbands were of their own choosing, against their friends' consent; for then they will be sure to make good their own folly.

FRANCIS BACON, LORD VERULAM (1561–1626)
Essay 'Of Marriage and Single Life'

THE JOY OF MATCH-MAKING

———— ‹‹‹❀››› ————

Miss Austen's Emma Woodhouse, unmarried and with time on her hands and a delight in coupling others, has seen her friend Miss Taylor wedded to a neighbour, Mr. Weston, and is talking to her father and another friend, Mr. Knightley.

'Emma knows I never flatter her,' said Mr. Knightley, 'but I meant no reflection on anybody. Miss Taylor has been used to have two persons to please; she will now have but one. The chances are that she must be a gainer.'

'Well,' said Emma, willing to let it pass, 'you want to hear about the wedding; and I shall be happy to tell you, for we all behaved charmingly. Everybody was punctual, everybody in their best looks: not a tear, and hardly a long face to be seen. Oh, no; we all felt that we were going to be only half a mile apart, and were sure of meeting every day.'

'Dear Emma bears everything so well,' said her father. 'But, Mr. Knightley, she is really very sorry to lose poor Miss Taylor, and I am sure she *will* miss her more than she thinks for.'

Emma turned away her head, divided between tears and smiles.

'It is impossible that Emma should not miss such a companion,' said Mr. Knightley. 'We should not like her so well as we do, sir, if we could suppose it: but she knows how much the marriage is to Miss Taylor's advantage; she knows how very acceptable it must be, at Miss Taylor's time of life, to be settled in a home of her own, and how important to her to be secure of a comfortable provision, and therefore cannot allow herself to feel so much pain as pleasure. Every friend of Miss Taylor must be glad to have her so happily married.'

'And you have forgotten one matter of joy to me,' said Emma, 'and a very considerable one—that I made the match myself. I made the match, you know, four years ago; and to have it take place, and be proved in the right, when so many people said Mr. Weston would never marry again, may comfort me for anything.'

Mr. Knightley shook his head at her. Her father fondly replied, 'Ah! my dear, I wish you would not make matches and foretell things, for whatever you say always comes to pass. Pray do not make any more matches.'

'I promise you to make none for myself, papa; but I must, indeed, for other people. It is the greatest amusement in the world! And after such success, you know! Everybody said that Mr. Weston would never marry again. Oh dear, no! Mr. Weston, who had been a widower so long, and who seemed so perfectly comfortable without a wife, so constantly occupied either in his business in town or among his friends here, always acceptable wherever he went, always cheerful—Mr. Weston need not spend a single evening in the year alone if he did not like it. Oh no! Mr. Weston certainly would never marry again. Some people even talked of a promise to his wife on her deathbed, and others of the son and the uncle not letting him. All manner of solemn nonsense was talked on the subject, but I believed none of it. Ever since the day (about four years ago) that Miss Taylor and I met with him in Broadway Lane, when, because it began to mizzle, he darted away with so much gallantry, and borrowed two umbrellas for us from Farmer Mitchell's, I made up my mind on the subject. I planned the match from that hour; and when such success has blessed me in this instance, dear papa, you cannot think that I shall leave off match-making.'

'I do not understand what you mean by "success",' said Mr. Knightley. 'Success supposes endeavour. Your time has been properly and delicately spent, if you have been endeavouring for the last four years to bring about this marriage. A worthy employment for a young lady's mind! but if, which I rather imagine, your making the match, as you call it, means only your planning it, your saying to yourself one idle day, "I think it would be a very good thing for Miss Taylor if Mr. Weston were to marry her," and saying it again to yourself every now and then afterwards—why do you talk of success? where is your merit? What are you proud of? You made a lucky guess; and *that* is all that can be said.'

'And you have never known the pleasure and triumph of a lucky guess? I pity you. I thought you cleverer; for, depend upon it, a lucky guess is never merely luck. There is always some talent in it. And as to my poor word "success", which you quarrel with, I do not know that I am so entirely without any claim to it. You have drawn two pretty pictures; but I think there may be a third—a something between the do-nothing and the do-all. If I had not promoted Mr. Weston's visits here, and given many little encouragements, and smoothed many little matters, it might not have come to anything after all. I think you must know Hartfield enough to comprehend that.'

'A straightforward, open-hearted man like Weston, and a rational, unaffected woman like Miss Taylor, may be safely left to manage their own concerns. You are more likely to have done harm to yourself, than good to them, by interference.'

'Emma never thinks of herself, if she can do good to others,' rejoined Mr. Woodhouse, understanding but in part. 'But, my dear, pray do not make any more matches; they are silly things, and break up one's family circle grievously.'

'Only one more, papa; only for Mr. Elton. Poor Mr. Elton! You like Mr. Elton, papa; I must look about for a wife for him. There is nobody in Highbury who deserves him— and he has been here a whole year, and has fitted up his house so comfortably, that it would be a shame to have him single any longer; and I thought when he was joining their hands to-day, he looked so very much as if he would like to have the same kind office done for him! I think very well of Mr. Elton, and this is the only way I have of doing him a service.'

'Mr. Elton is a very pretty young man, to be sure, and a very good young man, and I have a great regard for him. But if you want to show him any attention, my dear, ask him to come and dine with us some day. That will be a much better thing. I dare say Mr. Knightley will be so kind as to meet him.'

'With a great deal of pleasure, sir, at any time,' said Mr. Knightley, laughing: 'and I agree with you entirely, that it will be a much better thing. Invite him to dinner, Emma, and help him to the best of the fish and the chicken, but leave him to chuse his own wife; Depend upon it, a man of six or seven-and-twenty can take care of himself.'

JANE AUSTEN (1775–1817)
Emma, Chap. 1

BIDE AWHILE

I am my mammy's ae bairn,
  Wi' unco folk I weary, sir;
And lying in a man's bed,
  I'm fleyed wad mak' me eerie, sir.

  I'm o'er young to marry yet;
    I'm o'er young to marry yet;
  I'm o'er young—'twad be a sin
    To tak' me frae my mammy yet.

My mammy coft[1] me a new gown,
  The kirk maun ha'e the gracing o't;
Were I to lie wi' you, kind sir,
  I'm feared ye'd spoil the lacing o't.

Hallowmas is come and gane,
  The nights are lang in winter, sir;
An' you an' I in ae bed
  In trouth I dare na venture, sir.

Fu' loud and shrill the frosty wind
  Blaws through the leafless timmer, sir;
But if ye come this gate again,
  I'll aulder be gin summer, sir.

  I'm o'er young to marry yet;
    I'm o'er young to marry yet;
  I'm o'er young—'twad be a sin
    To tak' me frae my mammy yet.

ROBERT BURNS (1759–1796)
Songs

[1] Bought.

DR. JOHNSON SPEAKS

On Marrying Again

When I censured a gentleman of my acquaintance for marrying a second time, as it shewed a disregard of his first wife, he said 'Not at all, Sir. On the contrary, were he not to marry again, it might be concluded that his first wife had given him a disgust to marriage; but by taking a second wife he pays the highest compliment to the first, by shewing that she made him so happy as a married man, that he wishes to be so a second time.' So ingenious a turn did he give to this delicate question. And yet, on another occasion, he owned that he once had almost asked a promise of Mrs. Johnson that she would not marry again, but had checked himself. Indeed I cannot help thinking, that in his case the request would have been unreasonable; for if Mrs. Johnson forgot, or thought it no injury to the memory of her first love,—the husband of her youth and the father of her children,—to make a second marriage, why should she be precluded from a third, should she be so inclined? In Johnson's persevering fond appropriation of his *Tetty*, even after her decease, he seems totally to have overlooked the prior claim of the honest Birmingham trader. I presume that her having been married before had, at times, given him some uneasiness; for I remember his observing upon the marriage of one of our common friends, 'He has done a very foolish thing, Sir; he has married a widow, when he might have had a maid.'

Marriage Unnatural

On Tuesday, March 31, he and I dined at Glen Paoli's. A question was started whether the state of marriage was natural to man. *Johnson:* 'Sir, it is so far from being natural for a man and woman to live in a state of marriage, that we find all the motives which they have for remaining in that connection, and the restraints which civilized society imposes to prevent separation, are hardly sufficient to keep them together,' The General said, that in a state of nature man and woman uniting together, would form a strong and constant affection, by the mutual pleasure each would receive; and that the same causes of dissention would not arise between them, as occur between husband and wife in a civilized state. *Johnson:* 'Sir, they would have dissentions enough though of another kind. One would choose to go a hunting in this wood, the other in that; or, perhaps, one would choose to go a hunting, when the other would choose to go a fishing; and so they would part. Besides, Sir, a savage man and a savage woman meet by chance; and when the man sees another woman that pleases him better, he will leave the first.'

Below Her Station

A young lady who had married a man much her inferior in rank being mentioned, a question arose how a woman's relations should behave to her in such a situation; and, while I recapitulate the debate, and recollect what has since happened, I cannot but be struck in a manner that delicacy forbids me to express. While I contended that she ought to be treated with an inflexible steadiness of displeasure, Mrs. Thrale was all for mildness and forgiveness, and, according to the vulgar phrase, 'making the best of a bad bargain'. *Johnson:* 'Madam, we must distinguish. Were I a man of rank, I would not let a daughter starve who had made a mean marriage; but having voluntarily degraded herself from the station which she was originally entitled to hold, I would support her only in that which she herself had chosen; and would not put her on a level with my other daughters. You are to consider, Madam, that it is our duty to maintain the subordination of civilized society; and when there is a gross and shameful deviation from rank, it should be punished so as to deter others from the same perversion.'

s

MARRIAGE AND MONEY

He said, 'It is commonly a weak man, who married for love.' We then talked of marrying women of fortune; and I mentioned a common remark, that a man may be, upon the whole, richer by marrying a woman with a very small portion, because a woman of fortune will be proportionally expensive; whereas a woman who brings none will be very moderate in expenses. *Johnson:* 'Depend upon it, Sir, this is not true. A woman of fortune being used to the handling of money, spends it judiciously: but a woman who gets the command of money for the first time upon her marriage, has such a gust in spending it, that she throws it away with great profusion.'

RETORT IN KIND

I repeated to him an argument of a lady of my acquaintance, who maintained, that her husband's having been guilty of numberless infidelities, released her from conjugal obligations, because they were reciprocal. *Johnson:* 'This is miserable stuff, Sir. To the contract of marriage, besides the man and wife there is a third party—Society; and if it be considered as a vow—God: and, therefore, it cannot be dissolved by their consent alone. Laws are not made for particular cases, but for men in general. A woman may be unhappy with her husband; but she cannot be freed from him without the approbation of the civil and ecclesiastical power. A man may be unhappy, because he is not so rich as another; but he is not to seize upon another's property with his own hand.' *Boswell:* But, Sir, this lady does not want that the contract should be dissolved; she only argues that she may indulge herself in gallantries with equal freedom as her husband does, provided she takes care not to introduce a spurious issue into his family.' *Johnson:* 'This lady of yours, Sir, I think, is very fit for a brothel.'

JAMES BOSWELL (1740–1795)
The Life of Dr. Johnson
Entries of 1769, 1772, 1775, 1776

Mrs. Thrale Rebuked

Madam

If I interpret your letter right, you are ignominiously married, if it is yet undone, let us once talk together. If you have abandoned your children and your religion, God forgive your wickedness; if you have forfeited your Fame, and your country, may your folly do no further mischief.

If the last act is yet to do, I, who have loved you, esteemed you, reverenced you, and served you, I who long thought you the first of human kind, entreat that before your fate is irrevocable, I may once more see you. I was, I once was,

Madam, most truly yours.

Sam: Johnson.

July 2. 1784
I will come down if you permit it.

SAMUEL JOHNSON (1709—1784)
The Letters of Samuel Johnson

A WIFE'S CURSE ON COUNTRY LIFE

The hatred of squires' wives for the isolation and what they deemed the boorishness of country life was a familiar theme of the Restoration Drama. There is an early sounding of this grievance in the work of James Shirley who bridged the gap between the Jacobean and the Restoration stage. In *The Lady of Pleasure* (1637) Aretina, gay and extravagant, the wife of Sir Thomas Bornwell, having come to his house in the Strand, immediately announces her contempt for the world of Morris dance and Maypole and all that our Folk Dancers wish to recapture and preserve. Sir Thomas later decides to stop scolding and play her at her own game of urban extravagance and amorous intrigue. It is amusing to note the reference to the Traffic and Parking Problems and the complaints about obstructive coaches which had vexed the Elizabethans before Shirley's time; Dekker had complained of the 'thundering' noise of a 'world on wheels' in *The Seven Deadly Sins of London*.

Enter Aretina and her Steward.

Steward. Be patient, madam; you may have your pleasure.

Aretina. 'Tis that I came to town for. I would not
    Endure again the country conversation
    To be the lady of six shires—the men
    So near the primitive making them retain
    A sense of nothing but the earth, their brains
    And barren heads standing as much in want
    Of ploughing as their ground; to hear a fellow
    Make himself merry, and his horse, with whistling
    Sellinger's Round; to observe with what solemnity
    They keep their wakes and throw for pewter candlesticks!
    How they become the morris, with whose bells
    They ring all in to Whitsun ales, and sweat
    Through twenty scarfs and napkins till the hobby-horse
    Tire, and Maid Marian, dissolv'd to a jelly,
    Be kept for spoon meat!

Steward. These, with your pardon, are no argument
    To make the country life appear so hateful,
    At least to your particular, who enjoy'd
    A blessing in that calm, would you be pleas'd

To think so, and the pleasure of a kingdom.
While your own will commanded what should move
Delights, your husband's love and power join'd
To give your life more harmony. You liv'd there
Secure and innocent, belov'd of all,
Prais'd for your hospitality, and pray'd for.
You might be envied, but malice knew
Not where you dwelt. I would not prophesy,
But leave to your own apprehension
What may succeed your change.

Aretina. You do imagine,
No doubt, you have talk'd wisely, and confuted
London past all defence. Your master should
Do well to send you back into the country
With title of superintendent-bailie.

Steward. How, madam!

Aretina. Even so, sir.

Steward. I am a gentleman, though now your servant.

Aretina. A country gentleman,
By your affection to converse with stubble.
His tenants will advance your wit and plump it so
With beef and bag-pudding.

Steward. You may say your pleasure;
It becomes not me to dispute.

Aretina. Complain to the lord of the soil, your master.

Steward. You're a woman of an ungovern'd passion, and
I pity you.

Enter Sir Thomas Bornwell

Bornwell. How now? What's the matter?

Steward. Nothing, sir. *Exit Steward*

Bornwell. Angry, sweetheart?

Aretina. I am angry with myself,
To be so miserably restrain'd in things
Wherein it doth concern your love and honour
To see me satisfied.

Bornwell. In what, Aretina
Dost thou accuse me? Have I not obey'd

All thy desires, against mine own opinion
Quitted the country and remov'd the hope
Of our return by sale of that fair lordship
We liv'd in, chang'd a calm and retir'd life
For this wild town, compos'd of noise and charge?

Aretina. What charge more than is necessary
For a lady of my birth and education?

Bornwell. I am not ignorant how much nobility
Flows in your blood, your kinsmen great and powerful
I' th' state; but with this, lose not your memory
Of being my wife. I shall be studious,
Madam, to give the dignity of your birth
All the best ornaments which become my fortune;
But would not flatter it, to ruin both
And be the fable of the town, to teach
Other men loss of wit by mine, employ'd
To serve your vast expenses.

Aretina. Am I then
Brought in the balance? So, sir!

Bornwell. Though you weigh
Me in a partial scale, my heart is honest,
And must take liberty to think you have
Obey'd no modest counsel to affect,
Nay, study ways of pride and costly ceremony:
Your change of gaudy furniture, and pictures
Of this Italian master and that Dutchman's;
Your mighty looking-glasses like artillery
Brought home on engines; the superfluous plate,
Antic and novel; vanities of tires;
Fourscore-pound suppers for my lord your kinsman,
Banquets for t'other lady, aunt, and counsins;
And perfumes that exceed all; train of servants
To stifle us at home, and show abroad
More motley than the French or the Venetian
About your coach, whose rude postilion
Must pester every narrow lane till passengers
And tradesmen curse your choking up their stalls,

And common cries pursue your ladyship
For hind'ring o' their market.

(*Bornwell continues to indict her extravagance and gambling, to
which she replies:*)

Aretina. I'll not be so tedious
In my reply, but without art or elegance
Assure you I keep still my first opinion;
And though you veil your avaricious meaning
With handsome names of modesty and thrift,
I find you would entrench and wound the liberty
I was born with. Were my desires unprivileg'd
By example, while my judgement thought 'em fit,
You ought not to oppose; but when the practice
And tract of every honourable lady
Authorize me, I take it great injustice
To have my pleasures circumscrib'd and taught me.
A narrow-minded husband is a thief
To his own fame, and his preferment too;
He shuts his parts and fortunes from the world,
While from the popular vote and knowledge men
Rise to employment in the state.

Bornwell. I have
No great ambition to buy preferment
At so dear rate.

Aretina. Nor I to sell my honour
By living poor and sparingly. I was not
Bred in that ebb of fortune, and my fate
Shall not compel me to't.

JAMES SHIRLEY (1596–1666)
The Lady of Pleasure, Act 1, Scene I

CHRISTIAN MARRIAGE

The religious revolt against marriage is a very old one. Christianity began with a fierce attack on marriage; and to this day the celibacy of the Roman Catholic priesthood is a standing protest against its compatibility with the higher life. St. Paul's reluctant sanction of marriage; his personal protest that he countenanced it of necessity and against his own conviction; his contemptuous "better to marry than to burn" is only out of date in respect of his belief that the end of the world was at hand and that there was therefore no longer any population question. His instinctive recoil from its worst aspect as a slavery to pleasure which induces two people to accept slavery to one another has remained an active force in the world to this day, and is now stirring more uneasily than ever. We have more and more Pauline celibates whose objection to marriage is the intolerable indignity of being supposed to desire or live the married life as ordinarily conceived. Every thoughtful and observant minister of religion is troubled by the determination of his flock to regard marriage as a sanctuary for pleasure, seeing as he does that the known libertines of his parish are visibly suffering much less from intemperance than many of the married people who stigmatize them as monsters of vice.

The late Hugh Price Hughes, an eminent Methodist divine, once organized in London a conference of respectable men to consider the subject. Nothing came of it (nor indeed could have come of it in the absence of women); but it had its value as giving the young sociologists present, of whom I was one, an authentic notion of what a picked audience of respectable men understood by married life. It was certainly a staggering revelation. Peter the Great would have been shocked; Byron would have been horrified; Don Juan would have fled from the conference into a monastery. The respectable men all regarded the marriage ceremony as a rite which absolved them from the laws of health and temperance; inaugurated a life-long honeymoon; and placed their pleasures on exactly the same footing as their prayers. It seemed entirely proper and natural to them that out of every twenty-four hours of their lives they should pass eight shut up in one room with their wives alone, and this, not birdlike, for the mating season, but all the year round and every year. How they settled even such minor questions as to which party should decide whether and how much the window should be open and how many blankets should be on the bed, and at what hour they should go to bed and get up so as to avoid disturbing one another's sleep, seemed insoluble questions to me. But the members of the conference did not seem to mind. They were content to have the whole national housing problem treated on a basis of one room for two people. That was the essence of marriage for them.

G. Bernard Shaw (1856–1950)
Preface to *Getting Married*

PROPER CHOICES

The question of professions, in as far as they regard marriage, was only interesting to women until of late days, but it touches all of us now. Certainly, if I could help it, I would never marry a wife who wrote. The practice of letters is miserably harassing to the mind; and after an hour or two's work, all the more human portion of the author is extinct; he will bully, backbite, and speak daggers. Music, I hear, is not much better. But painting, on the contrary, is often highly sedative; because so much of the labour, after your picture is once begun, is almost entirely manual, and of that skilled sort of manual labour which offers a continual series of successes, and so tickles a man, through his vanity, into good humour. Alas! in letters there is nothing of this sort.

*

A ship captain is a good man to marry if it is a marriage of love, for absences are a good influence in love and keep it bright and delicate; but he is just the worst man if the feeling is more pedestrian, as habit is too frequently torn open and the solder has never time to set. Men who fish, botanise, work with the turning-lathe, or gather sea-weeds, will make admirable husbands; and a little amateur painting in water-colour shows the innocent and quiet mind. Those who have a few intimates are to be avoided; while those who swim loose, who have their hat in their hand all along the street, who can number an infinity of acquaintances and are not chargeable with any one friend, promise an easy disposition and no rival to the wife's influence. I will not say they are the best of men, but they are the stuff out of which adroit and capable women manufacture the best husbands. It is to be noticed that those who have loved once or twice already are so much the better educated to a woman's hand; the bright boy of fiction is an odd and most uncomfortable mixture of shyness and coarseness, and needs a deal of civilising. Lastly (and this is, perhaps, the golden rule), no woman should marry a teetotaller, or a man who does not smoke. It is not for nothing that this 'ignoble tabagie', as Michelet calls it, spreads over all the world. Michelet rails against it because it renders you happy apart from thought or work; to provident women this will seem no evil influence in married life. Whatever keeps a man in the front garden, whatever checks wandering fancy and all inordinate ambition, whatever makes for lounging and contentment, makes just so surely for domestic happiness.

R. L. STEVENSON (1850–1894)
Virginibus Puerisque